God's Hea

BOOK FIVE

The WAR DANCES of GOD

*The Shulamite Bride asks,
"Why would ou want to see me dance?"
The Bridegroom-King answers,
"Because you dance so gracefully,
as though you danced with angels,*
a sword-dance of joyous victory
as you whirl in **the dance of two swords**
between two armies."

—SoS. 6:13 tPt/BBE/Voice/CEB/NLT

JAMES M. MASSA

Copyright © 2021 James Mark Massa

The WAR DANCES of GOD

Printed in the USA

ISBN (print): 979-8-4811941-9-6

Photo Credit: Dancer on Front Cover by Dr. Pamela Hardy

Dr. Hardy is an anointed teacher and dancer. To connect with her, please visit www.eaglesiti.org.

All Rights Reserved. This book is protected by the copyright laws of the United States of America. This book may not be copied or reprinted for commercial gain or profit. The use of short quotations is permitted. Permission will be granted upon request. The author guarantees all contents are original and do not infringe upon the legal rights of any other person or work.

Design, layout, preparation for publication by:
Palm Tree Productions
www.palmtreeproductions.com

There are more than 100 different translations of scripture used in this work. A complete listing of all translations used is located in the Appendix. Abbreviations follow each reference to give proper credit for each version(s) of the Bible used.

TO CONTACT THE AUTHOR:

Sons of the Branch Ministries
6740 Richardsville Road | Bowling Green, KY 42101
270-777-8377 | sonsofthebranch@yahoo.com

DEDICATION

This book is dedicated to my second born son, Seth Josiah Massa. Like John the Baptist, Seth started dancing under the anointing of Holy Spirit while he was still in his mother's womb. He's still dancing today, and it is powerful.

THE SEVEN BOOKS IN GOD'S HEART OF WAR SERIES

Book One — *The War Songs of God*
Sing the War Songs of God against the host of hell. Declare the doom, defeat, and destruction of God's enemies.

Book Two — *The Lock and Load Prophecies of God*

Volume One — Sing the taunting War Songs, Wail the sarcastic Lamentations, and Chant the mocking Dirges as we attack, kill, and bury our demonic adversaries.

Volume Two — Destroy the strongholds of shame, arrogant pride, unforgiveness, and worthless failure with God's songs of deliverance.

Volume Three — Defeat the religious spirit of sorcery, sexual addiction, human trafficking, and terrorist's groups with God's songs of rebuke.

Book Three — *The War Cries of God*
Shout God's War Cries and see the walls of demonic strongholds fall. God's War Cry creates God's warriors, and warriors shout War Cries. Shout and release the roar of God's Lion!

Book Four — *The War Whip and War Flags of God*
>   Learn how the Whip and Flags are used in our warfare-worship to release God's deliverance, healing, wisdom, joy, unity, prosperity, and so much more over His family.

Book Five — *The War Dances of God*
>   This is a study of the various War Dances revealed in the Bible. As God's dances of war, they release the power and joy of God's Kingdom into the world.

The next two books are works in progress.

Book Six — *The War Horses of God*
>   Part One covers the revelation of Jesus' return found in Psalm 110. Part Two shows us why we must bring all our spiritual weapons together. When we do, it will produce God's War Horses which the Lord uses to destroy Babylon.

Book Seven — *The War Plans of God*
>   The War Plans of God is a review of His Seven Major Covenants. You will see that God's destiny for us has remained the same since creation. Under the lordship of Jesus and as His overcomers, we defeat the enemies of Jesus and fulfill His Four Great Commissions.

CONTENTS

USE OF RESOURCES IN THIS BOOK   ix

INTRODUCTION   11
WARRIORS OF GOD, IT'S TIME TO
DANCE A WAR DANCE!

CHAPTER ONE   19
GOD'S WARRIORS DANCE HIS WAR DANCES

CHAPTER TWO   29
GOD'S WAR DANCE OF FIRE
REVERSES THE CURSE

CHAPTER THREE   39
MIRIAM'S WAR DANCE CELEBRATED
GOD'S DELIVERANCE

CHAPTER FOUR   49
DAVID DANCED INTO GOD'S DESTINY

CHAPTER FIVE   59
DAVID'S WAR DANCE TO JESUS,
OUR WARRIOR-KING

CHAPTER SIX 71
War Dances Bind the Enemy with God's Chains

CHAPTER SEVEN 83
We Are Transformed into God's Stag

CHAPTER EIGHT 93
The War Dance of God's Majestic War Horse

CHAPTER NINE 105
The Bride's Sword-Dance of the Open Portal

CHAPTER TEN 117
War Dances Exalting the Messiah and His Salvation

CHAPTER ELEVEN 129
War Dances Rejoicing in Jesus' Healing Power

CHAPTER TWELVE 139
The Godhead Loves to Dance with Joy

CONCLUSION 151
Everybody Dance a War Dance Now!

MEET THE AUTHOR 175
James "Mark" Massa

USE OF RESOURCES IN THIS BOOK

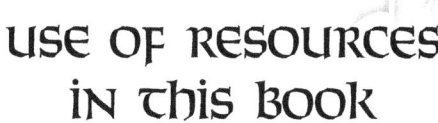

This Bible study on *The War Dances of God* utilizes what I call, *The Combined Translations Bible* (CTB, work in progress) technique. When I quote a verse from the Bible, I combine words or phrases from different Bible translations of that verse.

Here is an example from the book of Acts:

> *"Repent ye therefore, and be converted, that your sins may be blotted out, and completely taken away when the seasons of refreshing shall come, times of revival and recovery come from the presence of the Lord; that He may send Jesus Christ, which before we preached unto you:* **Yet He must remain in heaven, heaven must retain Him until the times of restitution and universal reformation of all things, the great Restoration** *which God has spoken by the mouth of* **all** *His holy prophets since the world began."*

> Acts 3:19-21 KJV/ASV/CW/AAT/BBE/RSV/Mof

In this verse I have combined words and phrases from seven translations to bring out the truth in God's Word in a more powerful way (Note: all words in bold print throughout the book are my emphasis). I may repeat a line two or three times to fully reveal what the Spirit of God is saying. Like the verse telling us Jesus *must remain in heaven, heaven must retain Him, until the great Restoration of all things* prophesied by all the prophets since the world began.

The *Combined Translations Bible* compares over 150 different English translations of the Bible (see the Appendix for a list of the Bible translations used for this book).

I also need to mention my "go to" resource I constantly rely upon to discover the meanings of the Hebrew words in the Old Testament. It is the *Hebrew Word Pictures* by Dr. Frank T. Seekins. He takes the original words of the Hebrew language which were in the form of drawings, or pictures (called pictographs) and gives the literal (letter-by-letter) definition of the Hebrew word. His work is full of revelation, and I highly encourage the reader to purchase a copy for their library.

INTRODUCTION

WARRIORS OF GOD, IT'S TIME TO DANCE A WAR DANCE!

Dancing is a universal expression of emotion. All over the world, every culture has some form of dance to express every type of feeling. We dance with joy as we celebrate life at weddings, holidays, parties, and games. People dance during times of worship, and some cultures even dance at funerals. Dancing in the physical realm can release an explosion of passion.

In this book, we'll study specific dances that originate from the spiritual realm. They are the War Dances from the heart of God. And under the anointing of the Holy Spirit, they release an explosion of God's power and glory in the spiritual and the physical world.

Throughout history, warriors have danced War Dances—*before, during, and after* the battle. They would dance *before* they went into battle to encourage and prepare their hearts for the stress and shock of combat. Warriors danced *after* the battle to celebrate their victory, and some armies *danced while they fought* because their dancing was a form of martial arts. An example is the fighting form called Capoeira of Afro-Brazilian origin.[1] Dancing is how they fought.

It is time God's Warriors learn God's War Dances. We dance not just dances of love to show our adoration to the Lord. We dance our War Dances of victory to bring God's power and Kingdom on the earth. We dance them before, after, and *especially* during our spiritual battles.

The Psalmist exhorts us to dance to express our love as we worship the Lord. *"Praise Him with the tambourine and dancing"* (Psa. 150:4 NLT). Many believers are responding to this call with beautiful *dances of love* to express their adoration of Him. But today, God is calling us to dance a *dance of war* as we go to battle. The Lord reveals His War Dances to everyone with an open heart, and as we dance them, our King is delighted. Solomon says our Bridegroom-King is pleased when His Bride dances for Him. And the dance that specifically blesses our King is a War Dance!

In the Song of Solomon, the Shulamite Bride asks her Lover, *"'[W]hy would You want to see me dance?' The Bridegroom-King answers, 'Because you dance so gracefully, as though you danced with angels, **a sword-dance of joyous victory as you whirl in the dance of two swords between two armies'"*** (SoS. 6:13 tPt/BBE/Voice/CTB/CEB/NLT). The dance the Bride dances for her Bridegroom-King is called *"the dance of the Mahanaim"* (SoS. 6:13 NET). We'll study this dance later, but for now notice our Bridegroom-King enjoys graceful, angelic dancing, and the dance that specifically delights the King is her *"sword-dance of joyous* *victory between two armies."* As the Bride of Christ, when we whirl with two swords between two armies declaring a joyous victory to Jesus our King, the dance we are dancing is definitely a War Dance. King Jesus loves it when we, as His Bride, dance it for Him!

> ## Our King delights in the sword-dance of joyous victory of His Warrior Bride.

We can dance without music, but dancing is a lot more powerful when musical instruments accompany it. War Dances release more power when united with music because *each musical instrument is a spiritual weapon that releases a specific anointing of God's power and glory as they are played!* Combining our musical weapons with our War Dancing is a synergy of God's power. His anointing and glory are exponentially multiplied on our War Dances. We'll see the glory of God cover the earth as we dance on the enemy's head in warfare-worship.

Dancing God's War Dances manifest His victory in our lives and for this world. But we're not just **expressing** God's victory; we're **releasing** His victory as we play His weapons of music and dance His Dances of War. God's calling His warriors to dance His War Dances as we go to battle to bring His Kingdom upon the earth. God's Kingdom is *"righteousness, peace, and joy in the Holy Spirit"* (Rom. 14:17 NIV). Dancing God's War Dances of victory are a powerful way to manifest and release the joy of God's Kingdom into the world. Let's dance and bring God's joy, victory, deliverance, and peace to every nation!

> ## Dance God's War Dances and bring the victorious joy of His Kingdom to the nations!

IT'S TIME TO LEARN THE WAR DANCES OF GOD

This is the fourth book in "God's Heart of War Series." It's a Bible study full of God's Word to encourage you as you go into spiritual battle. Remember, we don't go into spiritual warfare and fight *to get* the victory—Jesus has already given us the victory. We go to war and fight *to give* the victory to those who do not have it.

We give the victory by decreeing and confessing God's Word over our land. We manifest His victory by singing, shouting, playing, and dancing. God's throne is established on our praise and worship (Psa. 22:3). In God's presence, there is fullness of joy and peace.

This book is a Spiritual Military Handbook for God's warriors who sing, play musical instruments, flag, and dance as they enter spiritual warfare. It's *for everyone* who loves to praise and worship the Lord because this book reveals how we destroy the enemy's strongholds as we worship the Lord.[2] Our worship is often a battle, and today we increase the power of our warfare-worship by adding new weapons from God's heavenly arsenal (Jer. 50:25). Some of the most powerful weapons are the War Dances of God.

The battle is real. When Jesus cast out a demon, the Pharisees accused Him of being in league with Beelzebul (i.e., satan). They said, *"It's only by the power of Beelzebul, the prince of demons that this Jesus can cast out demons"* (Matt. 12:22-24 Voice/NET). After Jesus exposes their false and foolish accusation, He tells His disciples, *"You can't enter a strong man's house and rob him **until you first bind the strong man**, and then you can clean him out. One cannot rob satan's Kingdom without first binding satan. **Only then can his demons be cast out. This is war, and there is no neutral ground**. If you're not on My side, you're the enemy, and anyone **not***

***working with Me** to gather the people are making things worse and driving them away"* (Matt. 12:29-30 NLT/NKJV/TLB/MSG/BBE). There's a war raging for the hearts of the nations, and it involves binding the enemy, casting out demons, and destroying their stronghold on people.

This is what this book is all about, and not only is the battle real, it has intensified. In this spiritual battle, there is no neutral ground. We're either fighting to gather people into the Kingdom of God, or we're not.

As we live on earth, God calls us to *"occupy it"* until Jesus returns (Luke 19:13 KJV). The Greek word for occupy is *pragmateuomai,* which means "to carry on a business," but it is also a "military term" that refers to taking possession of an area.[3] We're all soldiers in God's Army (2 Tim. 2:3-4) and need all the weapons we can get. Now is the time to *"bind the strong man"* (i.e., satan), cast out any demon, and take back what the thief has stolen. We can bind the evil one because Jesus, *the Stronger One,* fights for us (Josh 23:3).

Today, the Lord is calling us to do *His business* and take back everything that was stolen from Him. What was stolen from the Lord are the people and the kingdoms of this world (Luke 4:5-6).[4] Our job description in God's Kingdom is to be *His Holy Ghost Repossessors* and return the people and land to Him. David declares, *"The earth is the Lord's... and all the people living on it belong to Him"* (Psa. 24:1 NLT/BBE). It's not just the earth, but all the people, the nations, the kingdoms living on it who belong to God, and we're called to bring them home.

This military aspect of *occupy* is found in the Old Testament when Caleb encouraged the Israelites to take the Promised Land. He spoke God's Word of victory, *"Let us go up at once and **occupy the land, for we are fully able to conquer it**"* (Num. 13:30 NRSV/NET with footnote). The Hebrew word for occupy is *yarash* and means "to occupy by driving out the previous tenants and possessing it in their place, to take possession of and inherit."[5] Caleb is reminding them of God's promise to give them the land of Canaan (Ex. 3:7-10). Caleb was a man of faith and knew God would fulfill His Word. Lord, give us the same faith to possess the land!

Jesus tells us, *"Go and make disciples of all the nations"* (Matt. 28:19 NKJV). Until Jesus returns to earth, our business is to occupy—to take possession of the whole world for Him, in His name, and under His authority. We accomplish our job of occupation by driving out the previous tenants. In this New Testament age of grace, we're not talking about people when referring to previous tenants. We're talking about demonic *"principalities and powers"* (Eph. 6:12), the spirits oppressing the people. These are the spiritual *strongmen* that Jesus, the Stronger One, must bind. Once their spiritual bondage is broken, the people are free to come to the Lord, fellowship with Him, and follow Him.

The Promised Land for Jesus' Bride is not just the physical land of the whole earth. It is the physical inhabitants, the people living on this planet. This is how we make all the nations on earth disciples of Jesus and train them to be His warriors, and *"The kingdoms of this world have become the kingdom of our Lord and of His Christ, and He shall reign forever and ever!"* (Rev. 11:15 NKJV). That glorious day has come upon us.

DANCE INTO GOD'S POSITIONS OF POWER AND AUTHORITY

I conclude with a vision a man shared with my brother. This man was in a meeting when a vision suddenly appeared before him. He saw a huge chessboard with chess pieces all over the board.⁶ One side represented the warriors in God's Kingdom of Light, and the other was the warriors in the kingdom of darkness. The way the pieces were placed on the board revealed the kingdom of darkness was overpowering the Kingdom of Light and was about to exact an overwhelming defeat upon them.

Suddenly the chessboard began to shake violently. God was shaking it. All the pieces began to jump around to different places on the board. It looked like they were **dancing** into God's assigned positions. When the shaking stopped, all the Kingdom of Light had to do was make one move, and it was "checkmate." The game was over, and God's Kingdom was victorious.

The Lord is going to shake everything that can be shaken (Heb. 12:26-28). The shaking is bad news for God's enemies (Isa. 13:13-14), but it is good for us (Acts 4:31, 16:26)! Let's *dance* and see God place us in His positions of power and hear Jesus announce in victory, "Checkmate," as He knocks the king of darkness prostrate, flat on his face. The Lord of glory proclaims the verdict, "Game over, you lose!"

Our world needs a complete Holy Ghost shaking and housecleaning. It's time to bind the strong man, break his hold over the people, drive him out, and destroy his kingdom. Today we take back everything and everyone because they all belong to the Lord. One way we drive out the previous tenants, the unclean spirits in the land, is by ***dancing to the sound of our musical weapons***. As we dance and play, God's powerful anointing is released into the spiritual atmosphere.

This is the focus of *The War Dances of God*. As you study, you'll discover God's divine purpose for His War Dances. Just as our musical instruments are His spiritual weapons of sound, God's War Dances are His weapons of motion. Mixing God's War Dances and musical weapons together, we'll see a demonstration of God's power and glory like we've never seen before.

Today is the day we play God's musical weapons and release His power through them. We dance the War Dances of God, reverse the curse, and defeat the enemy. Our dancing feet tear down demonic strongholds and tread on the devil's head. Dance with joy. Spin around with the two-edged Sword of God in your hands and declare God's victory. Holy Spirit is moving over all the earth and proclaiming, "Now is the time to dance a War Dance!"

Move into your position of power as you dance and tread on the devil's head!

ENDNOTES

1. Information on capoeira retrieved at: https://en.wikipedia.org/wiki/Capoeira.
2. One excellent source on how to conquer the high places, the strongholds of the evil one is the book *Invading Babylon*, edited by Lance Wallnau and Bill Johnson.
3. The Greek word *pragmateuomai* is Strong's G4231 at: http://www.blbclassic.org/lang/lexicon/lexicon.cfm?Strongs=G4231&t=KJV.
4. When the devil tempted Jesus in the wilderness, he showed Jesus *"all the kingdoms of the world at once,"* and said, *"All these kingdoms, all their glory, I'll give to You.* **They are mine to give because this whole world has been handed over, delivered to me"** (Luke 4:5-6 Voice/KJV). The whole world and all its kingdoms were given to satan when Adam and Eve submitted to his temptation and rebelled against God in the Garden of Eden. The kingdoms of the whole world were handed over to satan is a true statement. If this was a lie, Jesus would have laughed it off as a joke because it wouldn't have been a *temptation* to Him. It was true, but Jesus had arrived to get the whole world back, not by bowing to satan but by obeying the Father and doing it the Father's way.
5. The Hebrew word *yarash* is Strong's H3423 at: http://www.blbclassic.org/lang/lexicon/lexicon.cfm?Strongs=H3423&t=KJV.
6. In the game of chess two opponents move the chess pieces in a strategic manner to gain the victory. The game is over when one player corners their opponent's king so he can no longer move. The winner declares "checkmate" and the defeated king is knocked over on his side.

CHAPTER ONE

GOD'S WARRIORS DANCE HIS WAR DANCES

> *Let the sons of Zion rejoice in their King.*
> ***Let them praise His name with dancing,***
> *accompanied by tambourine and harp.*
>
> Psa. 149:2-3 NASB/NLT

GOD'S WAR DANCES ARE HIS WEAPONS OF MOTION

Everyone can dance, even if we have any physical restrictions. We can still tap our toes, snap our fingers, nod our heads, or just "dance with joy" in our hearts. As we begin studying God's War Dances, ask the Lord how you can *dance for Him* and bless His heart.

Warriors dance, but they are not known for dancing the ballet or a waltz. They are famous for their War Dances.

Throughout history, soldiers have danced War Dances.[1] They dance before going to war to prepare themselves for battle and dance afterward to celebrate the victory. Some even dance during the fight. As God's *dancing warriors,* we dance at all three times.

We dance *before* our spiritual battles, not just *to prepare* for the conflict but by faith *to declare* God's victory in advance. We often dance *during* the battle because sometimes dancing is how we must fight; then we dance *after* the battle to celebrate His victory.

Psalm 149 is about God's dancing warriors and reveals this truth. We'll study this song later, but for now, note it exhorts us to praise the Lord by singing a new song, dancing, playing drums, shouting, and waving our two-edged swords (Psa. 149:1-6). It is about spiritual warfare as God's warriors worship Him by dancing. We wave our swords before the Lord because we're going into spiritual battle, and as we dance *"the wild sword-dance"* (Psa. 149:6 MSG) before our heavenly Commander, something marvelous happens. While we dance, *we bind our spiritual enemies with chains* (Psa. 149:8). This is definitely a War Dance!

Our praise, music, and dance create God's spiritual chains that bind the enemy. God has given us the honor to bind the enemy with the spiritual chains we release as we sing and dance (Psa. 149:9)! Sometimes dancing is how we must fight to bring God's victory.

> God's warriors fight by dancing His
> War Dance that binds the enemy.

God's War Dances are His *weapons of motion.* Movement is critical in God's kingdom. The Lord is always instructing us to move—*to do* something. He told Moses, *"**throw down** your rod,"* and when it turned into a snake, God said, *"**Pick it up** by its tail"* (Ex. 4:3-4). At the Red Sea, the Lord told Moses, *"**Lift up your rod and stretch out your hand** over the sea and divide it"* (Ex. 14:16 NKJV). Later, when the Israelites were thirsty, God had Moses *"**strike the rock** and water will come out of it so the people may drink"* (Ex. 17:6 NET). This principle to *"be doers and not hearers only"* (Jas. 1:22), to obey God's command to move, is seen throughout the Bible.

In this New Testament age of God's grace, Jesus tells us to *"**lay hands** on the sick, and they will recover"* (Mark. 16:18 NASB) and *"**baptize people** in the name of the Father, Son, and Holy Ghost"* (Matt. 28:19). God uses our motions to release His power and glory. Holy Spirit was imparted *"when the apostles **placed their hands** upon people's heads"* (Acts 8:18 NLT). As members of Christ's body, we are God's hands and feet on earth (1 Cor. 12:21). Our actions of faith release God's power, and dancing includes a lot of action—a lot of moving our hands and feet!

If your fellowship does not dance, I encourage you to pray about this! Ask God to reveal to your leaders the importance of dancing. In this day of increased spiritual warfare, we need the power of God released through His musical weapons and War Dances. God's warriors will dance like wild men and women—like David. The Church will be known for Her War Dances.

The battle for the hearts of this world has intensified. As we go to war, we need all the weapons in God's arsenal, and that includes His War Dances. It's time to see God's promise fulfilled, *"as surely as I live, **all the earth will be filled with the glory of the Lord**"* (Num. 14:21 NIV/NET). *We go into spiritual battle to fill all the earth with God's glory.*

There was a period of history called "The Dark Ages" (the fifth to fifteenth centuries). This new era that we're entering will be a time of God's light as the earth is *"filled with the knowledge of the glory of the Lord, as the waters cover the sea"* (Hab. 2:14 NKJV). It will be the period of God's dancing warriors. As we obey Him and dance, I hear God say, *"the 21ˢᵗ Century will be known as **The Age of the War Dancing Church!**"* Now is a good time for your church to learn to dance!

> God says, "The 21ˢᵗ Century will be The Age of the War Dancing Church!"

TO "REJOICE IN THE LORD" MEANS WE DANCE

As we study the Hebrew and Greek words for dance, we'll discover God's purpose and power in His War Dances. The Old Testament is full of Hebrew words for dancing, but we miss this truth in how some of these words are translated into English. One example is the Hebrew verb *giyl* (pronounced gheel). In our English Bibles, it is translated as *"rejoice, be glad, or be joyful,"*[2] but the *Gesenius' Lexicon* says it also refers to *specific physical actions*. For us to rejoice, to be joyful and glad (i.e., *giyl*) also means we "dance, spin around, go in a circle, twirl, and leap for joy!"[3] When God tells us *to rejoice in the Lord, He means—dance*! And the specific way He wants us to dance (i.e., to rejoice) is not in some nice, slow dance. Yes, slow dances are great in their place. But when God uses this word *giyl* for rejoice, it means He wants us to dance by *spinning around, going in a circle, and leaping for joy!* This is biblical, godly rejoicing. If we are not dancing, we are not truly rejoicing!

The first time *giyl* is found in the Bible was when David brought the Ark of the Covenant into the tent he made for it. David appointed the Levites to minister before the Ark and praise the Lord (1 Chron.16:1-7). They sang, *"Let the heavens be glad,* **and let the earth rejoice, twirl (i.e., giyl),** *and let them say among the nations, 'The LORD is King!'"* (1 Chron. 16:31 LEB/NRSV/ERRB). It is a day of rejoicing for the Ark, which represents the presence of God, has returned to Jerusalem. The Lord has come to reign, for He is King. The heavens are glad, and all the earth is twirling, dancing, and rejoicing!

To "rejoice in the Lord" means we dance. We spin around, go in a circle, and leap for joy!

In the parallel passage of this event, we're told David danced (2 Sam. 6:12-15). We will study this story later; for now, note that David is leading the earth in rejoicing, in dancing to honor the Lord Who rules as King. Let's follow David's example and dance with joy for our God reigns!

David sang a song entitled *"God Rules Over All. A psalm of David* **when his kingdom was established** (Psa. 97 subtitle tPt). David declares, *"**The Lord reigns! Let the earth rejoice, twirl [i.e., giyl—dance, spin around, go in a circle, and leap for joy]!** A fire precedes Him as He goes, consuming [and] devouring all His foes. For You are Yahweh, King-God. The Most High God above all the earth, You are exalted above all other gods. Yahweh loves those who hate evil, He guards the souls of the devout,* **rescuing them from the clutches of the wicked**'" (Psa. 97:1, 3, 9-10 tPt/JB/KJV/ERRB). David sang this song of victory and danced *when his kingdom was established* because God had come to reign as King. This was a War Song along with a War Dance that celebrated God's triumph. Fire went out from the

Lord and devoured all His foes as God rescued His faithful ones from the clutches of the wicked one.

Today Jesus, *the Son of David, is establishing His kingdom* on earth, so it's time for us to sing a War Song and dance a War Dance! Jesus has rescued us from the wicked one. Just as fire went out from God and destroyed His enemies, Jesus is doing the same for us. Fire comes from the Son's presence, like it flowed from the Father, to rescue us from the wicked one.

Jesus said, **"*I have come to cast fire upon the earth,* *and how I wish it were blazing right now!*"** (Luke 12:49 NASB/MSG). God's Word is like fire (Jer. 23:29), and the fire of God's Word represents His *"fiery judgments"* (Jer. 5:14 NET). We dance like David because Jesus, the Son of David, is now establishing God's kingdom on earth! We dance as Jesus casts the fire of God's Word on the earth. Fire precedes Jesus wherever He goes and devours all His demonic foes as Jesus brings His salvation to the world and rescues them from the wicked one.

In six Psalms, David exhorts us to *"rejoice (i.e., giyl) in God's salvation"* (Psa. 9:14, 13:5, 14:7, 21:1, 35:9, & 53:6). God saves us by the blood of Jesus. This is why we go in a circle, spin around, twirl, and leap for joy as we dance a War Dance, rejoicing in our deliverance!

Over forty times in the Old Testament, *giyl* is used to tell us to dance. [4] We can't cover all these verses, so I encourage you to study them on your own, but here is one more example. It's the familiar verse: *"This is the day which the Lord has made;* ***we will rejoice, shall twirl (i.e., giyl—dance) and be glad in it"*** (Psa. 118:24 KJV/ERRB). Every morning we get to dance and rejoice because we didn't make this day; God did. Dancing—what a way to start the day!

One morning while I was writing this chapter, my wife and I woke up feeling sluggish. It felt heavy in the house and hard to get moving. We realized this heaviness was from the enemy, and I knew it was time to practice what I preach. So we started singing, *"This is the day that the Lord has made."* I grabbed Sharon, and as we danced, we sang, *"We'll spin, go around in circles, and leap, for this is the day You have made!"* That oppression and sluggishness melted away as we leapt up and down, spun around, and went in a circle. Dancing is a powerful habit to greet each morning—leaping and spinning because this is the day the Lord has made!

Dancing—what a way to start the day!

WAR DANCES: OUR FEET BECOME THE FEET OF FEET

Another Hebrew word that means to dance that we miss because of how it's translated in our English Bibles is *chagag* (pronounced haw-gag). Most English Bibles translate *chagag* as the phrase *"to keep or celebrate a feast,"* but it's a verb that means "to move or go around in a circle, hence dancing, to celebrate or keep a festival from the idea of leaping and dancing in sacred dances, to reel and be giddy like drunkards." [5] Just as the word *giyl* is translated *"to rejoice"* but also means "to dance," it's the same with *chagag*. When God says *to keep a feast (i.e., chagag)*, it means He wants us to celebrate it by *dancing, leaping, and going around in circles*.

We celebrate by dancing, and this dance of celebration is a quick and lively dance *of leaping and going around in circles*! We *reel* and *whirl* around so fast that we get *giddy* (i.e., dizzy).

We're so dizzy; we *stagger and nearly fall down like a drunkard*. We dance like this because we are *drunk* in the Holy Ghost and on God's new wine (Eph. 5:18). It's the dance of the *drunken warrior worshipper*. Now, this is how God's warriors dance and celebrate His feasts!

The Hebrew letters in *chagag* are *chet, gimel,* and *gimel* and can literally mean "the feet of feet that enter the inner room." [6] We need to study this definition in detail. *Chagag* does not mean when we dance any dance, our feet become the feet of feet and enter the inner room. When we chagag, we keep God's festival, dancing. When we worship Him in this way and enter His presence in the inner room, this kind of dancing turns our feet into the "feet of feet." The title "feet of feet" is like the titles: "King of kings" and "Lord of lords" concerning Jesus. They mean He is the ultimate King and supreme Lord. As we dance this dance of the *drunken warrior worshipper*, our feet become the "feet of feet," the ultimate and supreme feet on earth. They are perfect for treading on the enemy and possessing our Promised Land.

To keep and to celebrate God's festivals means we dance. *Chagag* gives the image of people "gathering together for a festival, usually in the form of a circle for dancing and feasting." [7] They "would gather together and dance in a circle. [8] We celebrate God's festivals by dancing in a circle. It's a form of worship as we enter the inner room—the Holy Place where God dwells. As we dance in honor of the festival, our feet become the most blessed feet in the whole universe. Why, because these dancing feet bring us into God's presence, power, and peace!

For now, we'll look at just one verse where *chagag* is used. It's when Nahum proclaims Israel's deliverance from their Assyrian oppressors; an important verse because it's a prophecy concerning the coming age of preaching the good news of the kingdom.

Nahum declares, *"Look, there on the mountains,* **the feet of one who brings good news,** *who proclaims peace!* **Celebrate your feasts (i.e., chagag by leaping and dancing).** *O Judah, pay your vows.* **For never again will Belial, the wicked one, invade your land; he is completely destroyed"** (Nah. 1:15 NIV/NASB/NLT/JB). Note Nahum focuses on *the messenger's feet*, not his voice. This person comes leaping over the mountains, the *high places* of demonic oppression, proclaiming the good news of peace to Israel. The high places are not an obstacle to him. The people experience peace because *"the wicked one"* has been completely destroyed.

Some translations say *"the Assyrians from Nineveh"* (NET/NLT) represent the wicked one. This statement is partially true, but the Assyrians were just the tool used. The force driving them was the devil. The Hebrew word for wicked one is *Belial* which Paul informs us is another name for *"satan, the evil one, the devil"* (2 Cor. 6:15 tPt/BBE/Phil). God delivered Israel from *Belial,* the false god who was behind the scenes ruling Assyria. This is a prophetic picture proclaiming the good news when Jesus would come, destroy the evil one, and save us all.

We can dance and celebrate our feasts (i.e., Passover and Pentecost) with Israel *"for Belial is utterly annihilated,* **and we are saved!"** (Nah. 1:15 JB/TLB). Jesus brought us His salvation as He fulfilled the Feast of Passover on the Cross and conquered death. Fifty days later, He fulfilled the Feast of Pentecost when Jesus, our resurrected King, poured out the Holy Spirit and His power to totally annihilate the evil one (i.e., *Belial*).[9] This is the good news of the kingdom. King Jesus has destroyed the kingdom of darkness, set up His kingdom, and we can't stop dancing!

Psalm 89 recalls God's covenant with David. The psalmist cries out, *"Blessed, happy are the people **who know the war cry.** **They firmly march along shouting with joy.** They live in the light of Your kindness. In Your name **they rejoice, twirl (i.e., giyl), and dance all day long.** **We can do nothing but leap for joy all day long;** for we know Who You are and what You do"* (Psa. 89:15-16 NABRE/EXB/tPt/NKJV/ERRB/MSG). People who know the War Cry (i.e., *"the joyful sound"* in KJV) are happy. These blessed warriors march, shout, and rejoice in the light of God's face. The word for rejoice here is *giyl*. It is translated: *"leap for joy"* (tPt), *"twirl"* (ERRB), and *"dance"* (MSG). When *we know who God is and what He does*, we'll rejoice. We'll dance, twirl, and leap for joy all day long!

Thank You, Lord, for Who You are and what You do. We will dance, twirl, and leap for joy all day long!

ENDNOTES

1. Examples of war dances are listed at: https://www.britannica.com/topic/war-dance.
2. The Hebrew word *giyl* is Strong's H1523 at: http://www.blbclassic.org/lang/lexicon/lexicon.cfm?Strongs=H1523&t=KJV.
3. Ibid.
4. The 44 verses where *giyl* is used in the Old Testament are: 1 Chron. 16:31; Psa. 2:11, 9:14, 13:4-5, 14:7, 16:9, 21:1, 31:7, 32:11, 35:9, 48:11, 51:8, 53:6, 89:16, 96:11, 97:1, 8, 118:24, 149:2; Prov. 2:14 (a warning against evil dancing), 23:24-25, 24:17; SoS 1:4, Isa. 9:3, 25:9, 29:19, 35:1-2, 41:16, 49:13, 61:10, 65:18-19, 66:10; Hos. 10:5 (evil dancing for a false god), Joel 2:21, 23; Hab. 1:15, 3:18 Zeph. 3:17, Zech. 9:9, 10:7). After reading all these verses we realize the Lord wants us to rejoice, but God especially wants us to rejoice by dancing!
5. The Hebrew word *chagag* is Strong's H2287 at: http://www.blbclassic.org/lang/lexicon/lexicon.cfm?Strongs=H2287&t=KJV.
6. Seekins, Frank T. *Hebrew Word Pictures: How Does the Hebrew Alphabet Reveal Prophetic Truth?* Copyright © 2012. p. 10.
7. Benner, Jeff A. *Ancient Hebrew Lexicon of the Bible.* Virtualbookworm.com Publishing, College Station, TX 2005. p. 117.
8. Benner, p. 118.
9. The third annual feast is the Feast of Tabernacles (or Booths). We'll dance and celebrate this feast when Jesus returns and we experience the end-time harvest of people.

CHAPTER TWO

GOD'S WAR DANCE OF FIRE REVERSES THE CURSE

But for you who fear My name, the Sun of Righteousness will rise with healing in His wings. You will be bursting with energy and go free, **leaping with joy** *like calves released from the stall.* **You will tread upon the wicked who will be like dust under your feet.**

Mal. 4:2-3a NLT/MSG/JB

THE WAR DANCE OF GOD'S FREEDOM

Malachi is the last book of the Old Testament and is a prophecy about the coming of the day of the Lord. At the prophecy's conclusion, God exhorts His children to return to Him for *"the day of judgment is coming,* **burning like** *a furnace. The arrogant and wicked will be burned up like straw on that day"* (Mal. 4:1 NLT). It's a warning for anyone who has strayed from the Lord—a day of fire is coming. Return to God. Get right with Him, so you'll be ready for that day.

Malachi's prophecy ends with a beautiful promise from God. *"But for you who fear My name, the Sun of Righteousness will rise **with healing in His wings. You will be bursting with energy** and go free, leaping with joy like calves released from the stall. You will tread upon the wicked who will be like dust under the soles of your feet** on the day I am preparing, says the Lord of hosts"* (Mal. 4:2-3 NLT/MSG/KJV/JB). This promise explodes with God's victorious power. It's a revelation of what the Father does as we dance His War Dance of liberty.

Jesus is *"the Sun of Righteousness"* Who comes with healing in His wings.[1] Jesus heals everyone who reverently fears Him. Jesus heals us of all our physical diseases and delivers us from all our demonic bondages. We're *"bursting with energy ... leaping with joy ... **like calves released from the stall. [We] will tread upon the wicked"*** (Mal. 4:2 NET/NLT). Not only are we healed, but we're also bursting with energy as we tread upon the wicked one! This verse is one of the best definitions of the War Dances of God: *when our dancing feet are treading upon the head of the wicked one.*

> A War Dance is when our dancing feet are treading on the head the wicked one.

The Hebrew word for released is *yatsa'* (pronounced ya-tsaw) and has many meanings: "to come out, break out, be delivered, and escape."[2] Its Hebrew letters: *yod, tsade,* and *alef* can literally mean "to desire and need the work of God's powerful arm."[3] These definitions explain why *"released from the stall"* is translated as ***"loosed from yokes"*** in the Septuagint. *Yatsa'* means we *desire the work of God's powerful arm* because we *need His arm to break* demonic yokes and *deliver* us from their bondage. We *escape* and are free to dance in God's liberty.

We express our freedom like young calves that have been bound up in a stall. We *"leap for joy, playfully jump around, and skip about. **We dance like frisky calves** [as we] frolic and gambol"* (Mal. 4:2 ERV/NLT/CSB/MSG/NLV/NIV/NASB/ASV). To gambol means "to hop, leap, jump, cavort, caper, prance, and dance a jig."[4] This is a wild, cut-loose dance. When we are delivered from demonic bondage, our joy will burst out in this wild War Dance!

The Hebrew word for all these dancing actions is *puwsh* (pronounced poosh) and means "to act proudly [in a positive or negative way], to grow up, spread out, spring about, and be frisky."[5] A few synonyms for frisky are: "to dance, gambol, cavort, skip, prance, leap, spring, hop, bounce, and jump."[6] This dance includes every possible movement we can think of to perform! I mean this; I challenge you to come up with a movement that is not on this list, but you can't use any technical terms like allegro, adagio, etc.[7] God has given us an unbridled, no-holds-barred, War Dance of freedom. This is great news for all of us with two left feet. I might not be a professional ballroom dancer, but I can hop, leap, jump, or just stand there and bounce. When we realize God has set us free, we'll dance the best we can like crazy!

> When God sets us free, we'll dance the best we can like crazy.

Dancing this wild War Dance of liberty *activates God's power.* As we dance, God says we *"'will tread upon the wicked for they shall be ashes, dust under the soles of your feet* on *the day when I do these things' says the Lord of hosts"* (Mal. 4:3 NLT/NKJV). As we dance, our feet trample on the wicked, for they've become nothing but ashes under our feet. The Hebrew word for wicked is *rasha'* (pronounced raw-shaw) and refers to one who is "morally wrong, lawless, and hostile to God."[8] Its Hebrew letters: *resh, sheen,* and *ayin* can literally mean "to experience the destruction of the Most High."[9] The evil one is the ultimate form of wickedness, and *he will experience* God's destruction (Rev. 20:10). The God of peace will soon crush him under our feet (Rom. 16:20), and the Lord's probably going to do it while we're dancing!

> Dancing this wild War Dance of Liberty activates God's Power!

The Son of righteousness has a two-fold work when He comes. For those who have a holy fear of Him, like the Sun, Jesus heals them with the rays of His glory. For the wicked, He comes as the Sun, *"burning like a furnace, and all the arrogant and all who do evil ... will be burned up"* (Mal. 4:1 JB/BBE). A day is coming when Jesus will come to earth as the Sun of Righteousness. The fire of the Son will heal and restore, or it will burn and destroy.

Everyone will experience God's fire because our *"God is a consuming fire"* (Deut. 4:24 KJV). Asaph declares, *"Out of Zion, the perfection of beauty, God shines forth. Our God comes and is not silent.* **Furious flames of a consuming fire go ahead of Him and devour everything in His way"** (Psa. 50:2-3 NRSV/NET/tPt//NLT). Malachi says our hearts will be full of a holy fear of God or full of wickedness. That condition will determine whether God's fire heals us or devours us.

Earlier in his prophecy, Malachi warns us that the Lord *"will suddenly come to His temple ... but who can endure the day of His coming?* ***For He is like a refiner's fire*** *and like launderer's soap He will sit as a refiner and purifier of silver;* ***He will purify ... and purge them as gold and silver***" (Mal. 3:1-3 NKJV). Paul alludes to this time and encourages us to be ready for that day of testing. He says our works of the flesh are like wood, hay, and stubble and will be consumed by God's fire, but our works from the spirit are like gold, silver, and precious stones will not be consumed. They will be purified by His fire (1 Cor. 3:1-15). The fire of God will test our works. "Lord, make us ready for Your day of fire."

GOD'S WAR DANCE OF FIRE REVERSES THE CURSE

The fire of God's furnace will purify us while making the wicked one worthless, just as Daniel's three friends survived Nebuchadnezzar's furnace and came out rejoicing. They were not burned; it was their bonds that were burned away. They did not even smell of smoke (Dan. 3:19-28). Like them, we come out rejoicing. We come out of God's fire dancing. We are set free and dance in our liberty.

It's the wicked who are burned to a crisp and become nothing but ashes under our feet (Mal. 4:3). The Hebrew word for ashes is *'epher* (pronounced ay-fer) and refers to "ashes, a symbol of worthlessness, and is related to the word for dust and earth."[10] Ashes are the perfect image of something worthless. This is how we picture the enemy—as worthless as dust and ashes.

This word *'epher* is also translated dust in other translations (see Mal. 4:3 CEB/GNV/ GNT/Geneva Bible/NABRE/NLT) and reminds us of the curse in Genesis. When Adam and Eve succumbed to the serpent's temptation and rebelled against

God, their actions released a curse on all three of them. God tells Eve her offspring will crush the serpent's head, but her pain in childbirth will increase (Gen. 3:15-16). God tells the serpent, *"You will crawl on your belly, and **you will eat dust** all the days of your life"* (Gen. 3:14 NIV). Snakes don't eat dust, but God's Word is true. So, who is this *dust* the serpent consumes?

God then turns to Adam and says, *"By the sweat of your brow you will eat food until you return to the ground, for out of it you were taken; **for you are dust**, and to dust shall you return"* (Gen. 3:19 NET). Adam is the dust—the food for the devil. Adam represents everyone who is in rebellion against the Lord. They are dust, open game for our adversary who *"like a roaring lion prowls around **seeking someone to devour**"* (1 Pet. 5:8 NASB/NET). But glory to God, because of Jesus, we are no longer the devil's food! On the Cross, Jesus nailed every curse to the tree of life (Col. 2:14). The Cross is the tree of life because if we receive its fruit (i.e., the body and blood of Jesus), we will live forever.

Remember how God *"in the front of the garden of Eden posted angelic guardians and a flaming sword flashing back and forth to guard the way to the Tree of Life"* (Gen. 3:24 JB/NIV/ MSG/NET with footnote). To get to the Tree of Life, the Cross of Jesus, we must humbly submit to God's sword of fire, His Word of fire. God's Word and fire cut and burn away every unholy thing in our hearts. In Jesus, we are made righteous and return to Him and His garden of delight.

The pattern of how the Bible is written is beautiful. In Genesis, the first book of the Old Testament, we're told about sin and its curse. Why the serpent eats dust, and the rebellious are the dust. But in Malachi, the last book in the Old Testament, God tells us how He's reversed the curse. He does it by the purifying fire of Jesus, the Sun of Righteousness.

Everyone who fears and honors Him is no longer dust; the wicked one is now dust. And by the blood and name of Jesus, we tread on his head.

This dance is a War Dance of fire. Jumping, skipping, and leaping are how we tread on the wicked like dust under the soles of our feet. This is a clear image of spiritual warfare. It is a powerful picture of our victory in Jesus, the Sun. Through Him, the curse has been reversed! We are no longer dust; the devil is. We are now sons and daughters of God. We are dancing warriors for our Warrior King!

> *In Jesus, we are no longer dust. The evil one is now dust and under our feet.*

Please don't misunderstand me. It is the blood of Jesus that has reversed the curse of sin and rebellion, not our dancing. We dance to express our joy, but dancing is God's weapon of motion. It's our act of faith that activates God's power to attack any oppression or heaviness that is the result of the enemy's lies. The evil one wants us to believe we are still under the curse. We are not! Jesus' sacrifice broke the curse.

As we step out in faith and dance, our bonds are broken. Jesus has set us free, and one of the most powerful ways to activate and live in that revelation is by dancing.

THE WAR DANCE OF GOD'S FIRE OF PENTECOST

Another verse in the Old Testament mentions calves dancing in Psalm 29, a song by David about God's glory and War Cry of thunder. It is "one of the loveliest poems ever written [concerning] God's majesty revealed in the last days."[11]

David exhorts us, *"Give unto the LORD the glory due His name. Worship the LORD in the beauty of holiness. The Lord's shout is heard over the waters; the God of glory thunders"* (Psa. 29:2-3 NKJV/NET/NIV). God is coming as our "Warrior-King," and "thunder is His battle cry."[12] Our God is *"the Lord of the storm"* (Psa. 29 subtitle JB). Our Warrior-King has a War Cry, and it is powerful!

David proclaims, *"The Lord's **shout of thunder** breaks the cedars. **The Lord uproots** the cedars of Lebanon. **He makes Lebanon skip, leap, jump around, and dance like a calf.** God's shout of thunder **spits out tongues of fire**"* (Psa. 29:5-7 NET/MSG/Har/Rhm/NASB). The Lord uproots the trees of Lebanon, so they are free to dance. The Hebrew word for skipping, leaping, etc., is *raqad* which we'll study later. Trees in God's Word often represent people (Mark 8:24), which means Psalm 29 applies not just to trees but also to us.

Cedars of Lebanon has a double meaning. One is negative, one is positive, and both are a reflection of us. Negatively, the cedars of Lebanon symbolize pride (Ezek. 31). But positively, they reflect righteousness. The Psalmist declares, *"Look how You have made the righteous flourish like a palm tree, **each one growing in victory, standing with strength like a cedar in Lebanon**"* (Psa. 92:12 tPt/KJV)! Solomon specifically needed the cedars of Lebanon to build God's Temple (1 Kings 5:1-11). Righteous cedar trees are a spiritual picture of the kind of people God desires to use to build His house.

Before we come to the Lord, we're walking in pride. When we meet Jesus in all His love and glory, we repent. Jesus does not reject us; He desires us to be His bride. By His blood, Jesus changes us from a cedar tree of pride to a righteous cedar tree *"growing in victory."* Jesus, like Solomon, takes our lives and uses us as His holy *cedarwood tree people* to build His House.

When the Lord shouts His thunderous War Cry, we start dancing like calves (Psa. 29:6). Notice what happens as we dance. *God's shout of thunder **spits out tongues of fire**"* (Psa. 29:5-7 NET/MSG/Har). God's War Cry, our War Dance, and tongues of fire go together.

When we hear the phrase *"tongues of fire,"* we automatically think of Pentecost. When the Spirit of God was poured out on the 120 believers, *"they saw what seemed to be **tongues of fire** that separated and came to rest on each one of them"* (Acts 2:3 NIV). Psalm 29 is directly connected to Pentecost, for "in Jewish synagogues, **this Psalm was read on the first day of the feast of Pentecost**" (emphasis mine).[13] Psalm 29 is a prophetic song declaring what the Lord would do on that day.

The *"sound like **the blowing of a violent wind** from heaven"* (Acts 2:2 NIV/NASB) was the War Cry of God as He blew out His Spirit and birthed His Church.[14] As God baptized them in His Spirit and fire, surely, they were dancing like freed calves on that day!

The writer of Hebrews says God *"makes His angels spirits and His ministering servants, **His priests, tongues of fire**"* (Heb. 1:7 NET/Wey/tPt with footnote). Filled with God's Spirit and baptized in His fire, every servant of God is a minister of His fire. Like calves who've gone through God's fire, we become calves of fire dancing God's War Dance of freedom. *"Before you know it the God of peace will quickly come and crush satan under your feet, stomping him into the dirt. Enjoy the best of Jesus"* (Rom. 16:20 MSG/ NASB). We *"enjoy the best of Jesus,"* surrounded by God's peace as we dance on the devil's head of dust. Dance God's calves of fire, dance!

David concludes Psalm 29 with a declaration of God's majesty and a call to praise Him. *"**God's shout of thunder** *sets the trees dancing. A wild dance, whirling; and strips the forests bare. **Everyone in His Temple shouts, 'Glory!'** Yes, the LORD sits enthroned as King forever, from which He rules the world. The Lord gives His people strength;* **the Lord blesses His people with His kiss of peace**" (Psa. 29:9-11 MSG/NET/NASB/tPt). As we dance, God gives us His power and blesses us with His kiss of peace. Yes, we will shout, "Glory!"

Dance God's War Dance of fire and reverse the curse!

ENDNOTES

1. Footnotes to Mal. 4:2 in the Nelson Study Bible with Luke 1:78.
2. The Hebrew word *yatsa'* is Strong's H3318 at: http://www.blbclassic.org/lang/lexicon/lexicon.cfm?Strongs=H3318&t=KJV.
3. Seekins, pp. 10-11 and Benner, p. 229.
4. Synonyms for gambol at: https://www.lexico.com/synonym/gambol.
5. The Hebrew word *puwsh* is Strong's H6335 at: http://www.blbclassic.org/lang/lexicon/lexicon.cfm?Strongs=H6335&t=KJV.
6. Synonyms for frisk at: https://www.lexico.com/synonym/frisk.
7. These are terms describing ballet movements at: Ballet Terms Dictionary - BalletHub.
8. The Hebrew word *rasha'* is Strong's H7563 at: http://www.blbclassic.org/lang/lexicon/lexicon.cfm?Strongs=H7563&t=KJV.
9. Seekins, p. 11.
10. The Hebrew word *'epher* is Strong's H665 at: http://www.blbclassic.org/lang/lexicon/lexicon.cfm?Strongs=H665&t=KJV.
11. Footnote to Psalm 29 in the Passion Translation.
12. Footnote to Psa. 29:2 in the NET Bible.
13. Footnote to Psa. 29:11 in the Passion Translation.
14. For a detailed explanation on God breathing the wind of His Spirit as a War Cry to birth the Church see Book Three of "God's Heart of War Series" entitled *The War Cries of God*, pp. 59-61.

CHAPTER THREE

MIRIAM'S WAR DANCE CELEBRATED GOD'S DELIVERANCE

*Then Miriam the prophetess, the sister of Aaron, took a tambourine in her hand; and all the women followed her with tambourines and **with dancing**.*

Ex. 15:20 NRSV/NKJV/NIV

AFTER WE'RE BAPTIZED IN WATER, WE DANCE

The story of God destroying Pharaoh and his army in the Red Sea is a powerful image of what He does for us at water baptism. Paul says, *"I don't want you to forget our history, dear brothers and sisters, what happened to our ancestors in the wilderness long ago. That our fathers were all under the cloud, all passed through the sea. As followers of Moses,* **they were all baptized in the cloud and the sea. They went through the waters, in a baptism like ours, as Moses led them from enslaving death to salvation life***"* (1 Cor. 10:1-2 NLT/MSG/NASB). Israel was baptized in the waters of the Red Sea as Moses led them from slavery to Egypt to a life of freedom in God. It is a beautiful revelation of what happens to us in the Spirit when we're baptized in water.

Water baptism does not save us. It is an act of faith and obedience to Jesus' command to be baptized (Matt. 28:19). Water baptism is not a new concept in the New Testament, but we don't often consider that the first baptism took place in the waters of the Red Sea in the Old Testament. This baptism manifested how God delivered Israel from bondage to Egypt, a biblical symbol of the world's ungodly kingdom. What the Lord did at the Red Sea for the children of Israel reflects what He does for us at our water baptism.

Pharaoh and his army represent the world, the flesh, and the devil that once held us as slaves. Like them, our old nature is killed and buried in God's watery grave. Paul explains, *"***For we died and were buried with Christ by baptism. When we are raised up out of the water, it is like the resurrection of Jesus.** *And just as Christ was raised from the dead by the glorious power of the Father,* **now we also may live new lives***"* (Rom. 6:4 NLT/MSG). Something supernatural occurs when we are baptized.

Paul calls baptism God's *"***spiritual circumcision** *not done by the hands of men, in* **the removal of the body of the flesh.** *It was* **a spiritual procedure** *by the circumcision of Christ,* **destroying the power of sin.** *For you were buried with Christ when you were baptized. And with Him you were raised to a new life* **because**

you trusted the operation of God, Who raised Jesus from the dead" (Col. 2:11 NRSV/NIV/ NASB/NLT/MSG/KJV). Baptism is *"a spiritual procedure"* and an *"operation of God"* where He takes His scalpel and cuts (i.e., circumcises) our old nature. Like Pharaoh and his army, our old nature is buried forever in that watery grave. Leaving it there, we arise and begin our new life walking with Jesus.

This transformation is why Moses led Israel in singing, and Miriam led the women in dancing. Their old life of bondage was over. At their baptism in the Red Sea, they saw their oppressors completely destroyed. Teach this revelation before someone is baptized; there'll be singing and dancing!

> When someone is baptized, there'll be singing and dancing!

MIRIAM'S WAR DANCE OF GOD'S VICTORY IN WATER BAPTISM

When Miriam led the women in dancing, they did not play cymbals, trumpets, or flutes. Notice they picked the correct musical weapon. They played their tambourines. Isaiah tells us as God's people beat their War Drums (i.e., tambourines), God kept time with the beat of their tambourines as He beat down their enemies (Isa. 30:32). We must use the right musical weapons as we dance specific War Dances.

The Hebrew word used here for their dancing is *mechowlah* (pronounced mek-o-law), and it simply means "to dance."[1] It comes from the root word *machashabah* (pronounced makh-ash-aw-baw), which is interesting because this root word means to "meditate, think, purpose, and plan."[2] As the water crashed down upon Pharaoh and his army at the Red Sea,

Miriam and the Israelites *meditated and thought* about what just happened. She and all the women saw the Lord's *plan*. God's *purpose* was to destroy their oppressors and set them free from their life of slavery. Set free, they can now walk with God in His new life of liberty. This is why they danced in victory!

> Set free from slavery, we dance in victory into a life of liberty!

The word picture definition of *mechowlah* (dancing) tells us what Miriam and these ladies were specifically thinking. Its Hebrew letters: *mem, chet, lamed,* and *hey* can literally mean "the revelation of being surrounded and protected by the mighty water and Rod of the Shepherd."[3] No wonder they danced! They received this *revelation* as they watched God tell Moses to stretch out the *Rod of God* and part the waters of the Red Sea (Ex. 14:16). They were *protected by Rod of the Shepherd* and safely walked through the Red Sea. Then God used those same *mighty walls of water* to beat down and drown the enemy. Israel's baptism in the sea *cut off* their adversaries forever as Miriam and the women of Israel danced a War Dance of freedom.

As we study where *mechowlah* is used in the Old Testament, we'll see it refers to a War Dance. But before we do, we need to remember a vital biblical principle: all the *physical battles* in the Old Testament where Israel fought *human* aggressors show what happens in our *spiritual battles* in this New Testament age as we fight our *demonic* aggressors.

Today, we don't go around killing people! Paul says, *"[W]e are not fighting against people made of flesh and blood, but against the evil rulers and authorities of the unseen world, against the demon-gods and evil spirits that hold this dark world in bondage. This is for keeps, a life-or-death fight to the finish against the devil and all his wicked spirits in the heavenly realms"* (Eph. 6:12 NLT/tPt/MSG). *"For our fight is not against any **physical enemy** but against the **spiritual army of evil** in the heavens,"* holding the world in bondage (Eph. 6:12 Phil/JB). People are not our enemy; wicked principalities and spiritual powers in the heavenlies are. This is an important distinction to remember, particularly as the world becomes more politically polarized and the media "demonizes" people. Remember who and what you are at war against!

The history of the Israelites serves to instruct and warn us (1 Cor. 10:5-13). For example, the battles Israel fought in the natural realm against physical people teach us how to win our battles in the supernatural realm against spiritual forces. They give us military strategies for victory. If we want to win, the foundational tactic for victory is *to be right with God*! When the children of Israel were right with God, they won. When there was sin in the camp, they lost.

We only go into battle if God commands us to go and is pleased with us. Before we fight, we must be right (with God). We build upon this foundation with the following five simple but critical military tactics which ensure triumph. We do the *what, why, when, where,* and *how* God commands us. As God's warriors, this is the only way we dare fight in spiritual warfare. We must comply with all five to experience victory.

Before we fight, we must be right.

David is an excellent example of God's warrior who followed these tactics. Before each battle, David asked the Lord about His battle plans and would not proceed until he knew God's what, why, when, where, and how of the battlefield (See 1 Chron. 14:8-16). We do well to follow David's example.

OUR WAR DANCE OF GOD'S VICTORY

This word *mechowlah* (dancing) is used after David defeated Goliath. *"When the men were returning home after David had killed the Philistine, **the women came out** from all the towns of Israel to meet King Saul with singing **and dancing (i.e., mechowlah)**, with joyful songs, **with tambourines** and with musical instruments. So, the women sang as they danced, and said: 'Saul has killed his thousands and David his ten thousand'"* (1 Sam. 18:6-7 NIV/NKJV with 1 Sam. 21:11 & 29:5). Like Miriam at the Red Sea, it's women who are dancing, and one of the musical weapons they play is the tambourine. The *mechowlah* is a War Dance accompanied by War Drums (i.e., tambourines) and War Songs to celebrate God's victory over our enemies.

Mechowlah is used when Jephthah was a judge of Israel. The Israelites were oppressed by the Ammonites, and God raised up Jephthah to deliver His people. *"Then the Spirit of the Lord came upon Jephthah and **empowered him**"* (Jud. 11:29 NIV/NET). When he attacked the sons of Ammon, *"the Lord gave them into his hands and gave him victory"* (Jud. 11:32 NASB/NLT). Jephthah *"struck them with a very great slaughter and thoroughly defeated the Ammonites ... So, **the sons of Ammon were crushed, brought down to dust, before the sons of Israel**"* (Jud. 11:33 NASB/NLT/BBE/Knox). Like Jephthah, when empowered by God's Spirit, we can defeat our enemies. They'll be crushed like dust under our feet. Holy Spirit gives us the victory in every battle.

When Jephthah returned to his house, *"his daughter – his only child – ran out to meet him **playing on a tambourine and dancing (i.e., mechowlah) for joy**"* (Jud. 11:34 NLT). More is going on in this story than we can cover in this book at this time. But notice that once again, it is *a woman* dancing a War Dance while playing *a tambourine* as she celebrates the Lord's victory over an enemy. Ladies, do you get the message? A few men may dance like David, but it's the women who really know how to dance! Women of God, please lead the way. Cut loose, and we men will try to keep up.

> Men can dance, but women can <u>really</u> dance!

THE WAR DANCE OF RESTORATION

The Hebrew word *mechowlah* in the Old Testament has a parallel Greek word used in the New Testament. It's the Greek word *choros* (pronounced ho-ros) which refers to a "choir, a band (of dancers and singers) who stands in a ring and dances a circular dance."[4] We get our English words choir and chorus from this word, but this choir doesn't just sing; they dance as they sing! It's so natural; the two go together.

This word is used only once in the New Testament and refers to a wonderful time of joy. *Choros* is found in the story of the prodigal son. When the father saw his son returning home, he *"raced out to meet him. He swept him up in his arms, hugged him dearly, and kissed him over and over with tender love"* (Luke 15:20 tPt). The father turns to his servants and cries out, *"'Kill the fatted calf. Let's have a feast and celebrate;* **for this son of mine was dead and has come to life again. He was lost and has been found.'** *So, they began to celebrate and have a huge party"* (Luke 15:23-24 NLT/NKJV/Voice/Knox). The heart of this father is a beautiful expression of the heart our heavenly Father has for us! If you've strayed from the Father, no matter what you have done, come back home to Him. When the Father sees you coming, *He will run to you* with open arms of love. The Father can't wait to embrace you with hugs and smother you with kisses!

When the younger son came home, the older son was out working in the field. *"When he returned home, he heard music (i.e., symphonia)* **and dancing (i.e., choros) in the house"** (Luke 15:25 NLT). The word for dancing is *choros,* and the word for music is *symphonia* (pronounced soom-fo-nee'-ah), from which we get the English word symphony.[5] It refers to a "unison of sound (i.e., symphony), a concert of instruments playing in harmony."[6] Everyone *with one heart* of joy was dancing and rejoicing at the younger son's return, everyone that is but the older brother. He refuses to join the party because he is full of jealousy and anger (Luke 15:28). This son is chained by a spirit of jealousy which bars him from feeling joy and dancing with everyone at the party.

The older brother based his relationship with his father on his *works.* He complains to his father, *"All these years I have been* ***working like a slave*** *for you. I have* ***never disobeyed one of your commandments"*** (Luke 15:29 TCNT/tPt/Mont/KJV). The older brother was living the life of a slave, bound by dead religious works. Like some believers, he was living in legalism, obeying the dead letter of the law and not a new life of love in the Spirit (Rom. 7:6). Both sons needed a revelation of the Father's love, grace, and forgiveness.

The older brother is in worse shape than his younger brother. Jealousy and a religious spirit kept him from enjoying God's grace on himself and others. If he turned from his works *as a slave* and came to the Father's grace *as a son,* he could dance and have a party every day!

When the younger son came home, it's like he was getting saved and baptized. His father tells his older brother, *"Isn't it right to join in the celebration and be happy? This is your brother we are talking about.* **He was once dead and gone, but now he's alive and back with us again.** *He was lost but now he is found!"* (Luke 15:32 Voice/tPt). The younger son repented, and like being baptized in water, he was raised from death to life. Whether living like the wasteful younger brother or walking in dead, religious works like the older brother, it is time to dance whenever a wayward child of God returns to the Father!

Recall *mechowlah* is a derivative of the word *machashabah* which means to meditate, think, plan, etc. Both come from the root word *chashab* (pronounced haw-shab), which means "to think, meditate, plan, calculate, imagine, devise, and be mindful of."[7] This root word applies to *weaving or plaiting* and to think out something like *composing a song*. The image created by this word is that as we think and meditate on God, we'll compose a picture of Who He is and what He has done for us. If we have an accurate image of the Father—like the younger brother—we'll dance. If we have an inaccurate picture of the Father—like the older brother—we won't dance. We won't even be willing to go into the house where they're dancing. When we have a true revelation of the heart of the Father and His deliverance for us in Jesus, we'll be the first to dance a War Dance of victory!

WAR DANCES AND PROPHECY

I have one last comment concerning the *mechowlah* War Dance. There is a village in the land owned by the tribe of Issachar named Abel-meholah. This name is a compound word that means "the meadow of dancing."[8] What is interesting about this city is that it is the birthplace of the prophet Elisha (1 Kings 19:16). It is not an accident that the prophet came from the town of dancing. Jesus was born in Bethlehem, which literally means "the city of bread," and would feed the world the Bread of Life. In the same way, Elisha was born in the city of dancing and brought forth prophetic dancing. Some would say this is stretching the Word of God, but I disagree.[9] As we step out and dance, there's going to be a greater outpouring of God's Spirit of prophecy on His children! Believe it. Decree it. Get ready for it.

ENDNOTES

1. The Hebrew word *mechowlah* is Strong's H4246 at: http://www.blbclassic.org/lang/lexicon/lexicon.cfm?Strongs=H4246&t=KJV.
2. The Hebrew word *machashabah* is Strong's H4284 at: http://www.blbclassic.org/lang/lexicon/Lexicon.cfm?Strongs=H4284&t=KJV.
3. Seekins, pp. 10-11.
4. The Greek word *choros* is Strong's G5525 at: www.blbclassic.org/lang/lexicon/lexicon.cfm?strongs=G5525&t=KJV.
5. The Greek word *symphonia* is Strong's G4858 at: http://www.blbclassic.org/lang/lexicon/lexicon.cfm?Strongs=G4858&t=KJV.
6. Ibid.
7. The Hebrew root word *chashab* is Strong's H2803 at: http://www.blbclassic.org/lang/lexicon/lexicon.cfm?Strongs=H2803&t=KJV.
8. The word Abelmeholah is Strong's H65 at: www.blbclassic.org/lang/lexicon/lexicon.cfm?Strongs=H65&t=KJV.
9. It is not an accident that of all the prophets in the Old Testament it was Elisha who requested a minstrel to play so he would receive the prophetic word for Jehoshaphat the king of Judah (2 Kings 3:15) Music and dancing go together.

CHAPTER FOUR

DAVID DANCED INTO GOD'S DESTINY

> *David, wearing a linen ephod, a priestly garment,* **danced whirling around and round before the Lord with all his might.**
>
> 2 Sam. 6:14 NIV/NLT/JB/Sprl

IN GOD'S PRESENCE, WE DANCE WITH ALL OUR MIGHT

In one short passage of Scripture, Paul compares us to a warrior fighting a battle, an athlete competing in a contest, and a farmer planting seeds for a new harvest (2 Tim. 2:1-7). All three activities demand physical strength and endurance. One way to get in shape and stay in shape is dancing. God wants His soldiers strong in spirit, soul, *and body* like David—the ultimate dancing warrior.

David loved to dance. When the Ark of the Covenant was returned to Jerusalem, *"David, wearing a linen ephod, a priestly garment,* **danced whirling around and round before the Lord with all his might"** (2 Sam. 6:14 NIV/NLT/JB/Sprl). The Hebrew word here for danced is *karar* (pronounced kaw-rar) and means "to dance, to whirl, go around in a circle, to run and leap."[1] Its Hebrew letters: *kaf, resh,* and *resh* can literally mean "to open (the way) for the Most High of the most high."[2] As David whirled around, he opened the way for the Lord of lords to come into the city. The Israelites said the Ark of the Covenant was God's "war chariot."[3] As David danced before the Lord, the people saw God riding His war chariot into Jerusalem.

We need to see the context of this story. David was dancing a War Dance because he was waging a spiritual battle. King Saul had ruled Jerusalem while he was oppressed by demonic spirits. For years Saul's jealousy led him to attempt to kill David. During Saul's reign, unclean spirits had flowed out from Israel's king and polluted the whole city. Saul went from bad to worse as he sought the help of a witch (1 Sam. 28:4-25). After Saul died, the stronghold of those unholy spirits remained in the city. As David returned the Ark of the Covenant to Jerusalem, he and his army of praisers shouted a War Cry, sounded a Shofar, and danced a War Dance. Their warfare-worship drove out those demonic spirits.

David led his army in worship before the Lord. As they worshipped, they *attacked* the unclean spirits camped in Jerusalem! The parallel passage is found in 1 Chronicles, and it says David came with *"the leaders of Israel* **and the commanders of thousands, the generals of the army"** to bring the Ark to Jerusalem (1 Chron. 15:25 JB/NLT). What was his army doing as they marched into town? *"David and* *all the house of Israel were bringing up the Ark of the Lord* **with shouting and sounding the Shofar, the ram's horn trumpet"** (2 Sam. 6:15 NASB /NET with footnote). The Hebrew word for shouting is *teruw 'ah* (pronounced ter-oo-ah) and is a "war cry or battle cry."[4] David and his army were fighting for the heart of Jerusalem.

These are the *exact tactics* Joshua and the army of Israel used when they attacked Jericho. **"The ram's horn (i.e., Shofar) sounded***, and when the army heard the signal,* **they shouted a mighty war cry, a loud battle cry (i.e., *teruw 'ah*).** *The walls collapsed, and the warriors charged straight in and captured the city"* (Josh. 6:20 NET/ JB/NIV). Like Joshua, David led his army as they shouted their War Cry, "Ter-oo-ah!" and sounded the Shofar, their War Horn.[5] Like Joshua taking Jericho, David was coming to restore Jerusalem back to God.

> David attacked Jerusalem just like Joshua attacked the city of Jericho!

Walls were falling, but it wasn't *physical walls*. The walls that fell in Jerusalem were the walls of the demonic stronghold of jealousy, murder, and sorcery around Jerusalem. They were shattered by David's dancing, which was a spiritual battering ram. We discover this revelation in a derivative of *karar*, which is used to describe David's dancing. A derivative is the word *kar*, which refers to a "palanquin, a pasture, a ram, or battering ram."[6] *Kar* is translated as a *"battering ram"* twice in Ezekiel (4:2 and 21:22). As David whirled around in a circle, as he leaped, whirled, and ran, his dance became a spiritual battering ram knocking demonic walls down. O Lord, raise up godly leaders like David to stand against evil in our government today!

The strategy David used also applies to us for spiritual warfare today. If our city is infected with ungodly spirits of wickedness, we need to inquire of the Holy Ghost what to do. He may tell us it's time to blow our Shofars, shout our War Cries, and dance our War Dances. He may guide us to knock those demonic strongholds down with our *dancing battering ram*. And when we dance, we should dance like David. We should dance with all our might, like a wild man who doesn't care who's watching!

> As David whirled, leaped, and ran, his dance became a battering ram.

David did not hold back when he danced "[A]*s the Ark of the Lord entered the City of David, Saul's daughter Michal looked out the window. When she saw* **King David jumping, skipping, hopping, leaping (i.e., pazaz) and spinning, whirling, dancing (i.e., karar)** *before the Lord, she despised him in her heart*" (2 Sam. 6:16 NLT/NET/NIV/CEV/WYC/CJB/NKJV). This verse adds another Hebrew word to describe David's dancing. It is *pazaz* (pronounced paw-zaz) and means "to leap for joy, to bound, be strong, to be light, nimble, and agile, and to spring up as a gazelle."[7] Different translations of this verse reveal David is a wild man. Exploding with joy, David *springs up* like God's *strong and nimble gazelle*. He *jumps, skips, hops, leaps, spins, and whirls* in his dance. I get dizzy just reading about David's dancing!

WAR DANCES IRRITATE RELIGIOUS SPIRITS

The word picture definition of *pazaz* reveals what's going on here with David and Michal. Its Hebrew letters: *pey, zayin,* and *zayin* can literally mean "to present the weapon of weapons (or the sword of swords)."[8] In spiritual warfare, our War Dance is a weapon. It's like a sword that cuts through the demonic smoke screen and reveals what is hidden behind the haze of religious deception. This is what happened when Michal mocked David's dancing.

As Saul's daughter, Michal was infected by the unholy spirits that were on her father, and as a result, she despised David (2 Sam. 6:16). David's wild Holy Ghost dancing was like a sword that cut away the veil and exposed Michal's critical heart. Because she did not repent of her condemnation, she had *"no children to the day of her death"* (2 Sam. 6:23 KJV). If she had repented, Michal would have been healed. This serves as a warning for us. One of the consequences of a religious spirit that condemns Holy Ghost dancing is barrenness. It could be physical barrenness, spiritual barrenness, or it could be both.

DAVID DANCED HIS WAY INTO GOD'S DESTINY

The 1 Chronicles passage about David's dancing as the Ark returns to Jerusalem uses two new words to give us more revelation about the kind of dancing that pleases the Lord. *"As the Ark of the Lord's Covenant entered the City of David, Michal, Saul's daughter watched from a window. And when she saw King David* **skipping about, leaping, jumping, dancing ecstatically (i.e., raqad) and cavorting, spinning, laughing, and leaping for joy (i.e., sachaq),** *she despised him and was filled with contempt"* (1Chon. 15:29 NET/Amp/NLJV/ISV/NIV/NLT/MEV/MSG). The Hebrew words are *raqad* and *sachaq*. We'll study *raqad* first and then *sachaq*.

The word *raqad* (pronounced raw-kad) is translated as leaping, jumping, dancing, etc., and means "to stomp the ground with one's feet, to dance by skipping, springing, and leaping."[9] The primary imagery of *raqad* is to trample the ground with our feet. It's a beautiful depiction of our victory in Jesus that we acquire through our feet as we dance.

The Hebrew letters of *raqad* reveal what happens in the spiritual realm as we dance. Its letters: *resh, qof,* and *dalet* can literally mean "to enter the door (or to walk the pathway) into the destiny of the Most High."[10] As David danced, he entered the door into God's destiny. He was dancing on the pathway of God's destiny!

David was no longer running for his life from Saul. As he danced, his feet were stomping those demonic spirits of jealousy, murder, and sorcery into the ground. David entered into God's destiny as he danced because he was bringing the Ark, the presence of God, back into Jerusalem.

What a glorious image of what happens as we dance! When someone says they don't know what God's destiny is for their life, I ask them, "When is the last time you danced?" And I don't mean dancing downtown at the club, but dancing with joy and total abandon before the Lord. In that kind of atmosphere, God is able to reveal His destiny for you.

> David danced into God's destiny!
> When is the last time you danced?

When someone says, "I don't know my *life-dream*," I like to go even further, and I encourage them by asking, "Have you asked the Lord, 'What are Your dreams?'" When we dedicate our hearts to finding and fulfilling God's dreams, we'll find His dreams for our life.

DAVID'S WAR DANCE OF MOCKING LAUGHTER

The other word found in 1 Chronicles describing David's dancing is *sachaq* (pronounced saw-hak), translated as *"cavorting, spinning, laughing, and leaping for joy."* This word refers to a specific type of laughter. *Sachaq* means "to laugh in contempt, to mock, deride, scorn, to joke and jest (i.e., laugh repeatedly), and to dance."[11] David danced his War Dance of victory with *mocking laughter*. He couldn't stop dancing and laughing.

David wrote Psalm 2 (see Acts 4:24-26) and told us why he laughed as he danced. David knew God laughs at His enemies. David uses *sachaq* to describe God's reaction when the kings and rulers of the earth plot against Him and Jesus, *"His Anointed One"* (Psa. 2:2 Rhm). David says, ***"The One enthroned in heaven laughs (i.e., sachaq) in disgust****. My Lord will **mock their madness** and hold them in derision"* (Psa. 2:4 NET/Rhm/tPt). David watched the Father and Son laugh at the madness of those who tried to attack them. David learned to laugh with them at his enemies because God had given David the revelation of His grace in the New Covenant.[12] When we realize that we've *"been raised up with Christ,"* Who is *"seated at the right hand of God"* (Col. 3:1 NASB), we can join the Lord and laugh with Him. Together we can laugh at our enemies.

God really enjoys laughing at His enemies. Again David says, *"Evil men plot against the godly and viciously attack them,* ***but the Lord laughs (i.e., sachaq) in disgust at the wicked, for He sees their judgment day of doom is coming"*** (Psa. 37:12-13 NET/NIV/Mof). David uses the word *sachaq* for laughing and dancing to describe God's reaction to their attack on His godly ones. The wicked don't stand a chance against our dancing, laughing God.

When King Saul sent soldiers to David's house to kill him (Psa. 59 KJV subtitle), David cries out to God for help, *"Rescue me from my enemies, my God, protect me from those attacking me"* (Psa. 59:1 JB). David trusts God to save him, and what does the Lord do? He laughs! *"But You, Lord,* **simply break out laughing (i.e., sachaq) at their plans**. *You mock at all those hostile nations [who] are as nothing. You treat all those godless nations like jokes"* (Psa. 59:8 tPt/Har/ ABPS/Knox/MSG/NLT). In all these Psalms, David uses the word *sachaq* as God laughs at the wicked plans of the devil. Laughing with God at our enemy is our ultimate position of victory.

The word picture definition of *sachaq* gives more revelation concerning this War Dance. Its Hebrew letters: *sheen, chet,* and *qof* can literally mean "protected and surrounded by (God's) destiny destroys (our enemies)."[13] As he danced this War Dance of victory, David not only entered into God's destiny (i.e., *raqad*); the Lord's destiny surrounded and protected him (i.e., *sachaq*). From this position of safety, God's mocking laughter exploded upon David's enemies. Like David, let's walk in God's destiny and be protected. This assurance is why we can laugh, and this is why we dance with all our might!

David was the consummate dancer. The Holy Spirit needed to use four Hebrew words (i.e., *karar* and *pazaz* in 2 Sam. 6:16, and *raqad* and *sachaq* in 1 Chron. 15:29) to describe his dancing and reveal what was happening in the Spirit as David danced. Lord, anoint us with Your Spirit to dance. Raise us up to be Your Army of dancing warriors who dance like David!

Lord, anoint us with Your Spirit to dance.

God, raise us up to be Your Army of dancing warriors! As God's dancing warriors, let's dance like David:

- We **perform** the *karar* dance by whirling, going around in a circle, and leaping, which *opens the way for the Most High God to enter* into our worship. The Lord uses our dancing like a *battering ram* to knock down demonic walls!

- We **celebrate** the *pazaz* dance *leaping for joy like a strong, nimble gazelle.* Our dance becomes the *weapon of weapons.* Our dance of joy is the sword in God's hand that cuts away the deception and depression of the wicked one.

- We **rejoice** in the *raqad* dance as we *leap, jump, and stomp the ground with our feet.* We trample the enemy and shatter his lies under our feet. As we dance, *we enter through the door into God's destiny.*

- We **exalt** in the *sachaq* dance by *spinning, leaping, and laughing.* We laugh at the devil with our heavenly Father because, in this dance, we are *protected and surrounded by God's destiny that destroys* our adversaries. Yes, we will dance like David!

ENDNOTES

1. The Hebrew word *karar* is Strong's H3769 at: www.blbclassic.org/lang/lexicon/lexicon.cfm?Strongs=H3769&t=KJV.
2. Seekins, pp. 10-11.
3. Footnote to Num. 10:35-36 in the Jewish Study Bible.
4. The Hebrew word *teruw 'ah* is Strong's H8643 at: http://www.blbclassic.org/lang/lexicon/lexicon.cfm?Strongs=H8643&t=KJV.
5. For more information concerning the War Cry, Te-roo-ah, see Book Three of "God's Heart of War Series" entitled *The War Cries of God*, pp. 97-128.
6. The Hebrew word *kar* is Strong's H3733 at: www.blbclassic.org/lang/lexicon/lexicon.cfm?Strongs=H3733&t=KJV.
7. The Hebrew word *pazaz* is Strong's H6339 at: http://www.blbclassic.org/lang/lexicon/lexicon.cfm?Strongs=H6339&t=KJV.
8. Seekins, pp. 10-11.
9. The Hebrew word *raqad* is Strong's H7540 at: http://www.blbclassic.org/lang/lexicon/lexicon.cfm?Strongs=H7540&t=KJV.
10. Seekins, pp. 10-11.
11. The Hebrew word *sachaq* is Strong's H7832 at: http://www.blbclassic.org/lang/lexicon/lexicon.cfm?Strongs=H7832&t=KJV.
12. David walked in the revelation of God's grace in His New Covenant. David had this revelation. It's the only way to explain what he did with the Ark of the Covenant. David put the Ark in his tent (2 Sam. 6:17). He took the Holy of holies out of the Tabernacle and placed it in his tent. But God had established many rules concerning how the people of Israel were to serve Him before the Ark, and David broke every one of them! Only the High Priest of the tribe of Levi could enter the Holy of holies. David was of the tribe of Judah and was not a priest much less the High Priest. He was a soldier. The High Priest could only come in with a sacrifice of blood. David entered with sacrifices of praise. And last of all only one person, the High Priest, could enter into the Holy of holies one day a year. David went in and took many musicians and singers with him to worship the Lord, not one day but every day for 24 hours, all day long! David and all these people should have been struck dead by the hand of God the second they entered that tent. They weren't for David knew about God's New Covenant of mercy and grace in the blood of Jesus.
13. Seekins, pp. 10-11.

CHAPTER FIVE

DAVID'S WAR DANCE TO JESUS, OUR WARRIOR-KING

*David, wearing a linen ephod, a priestly garment, **danced whirling around and round before the Lord with all his might**.*

2 Sam. 6:14 NIV/NLT/JB/Sprl

DAVID'S WAR PSALM OF THE TRIUMPHANT KING

Psalm 68 is one of David's most powerful War Psalms. It declares the victory we have in Jesus, our resurrected King. We'll only cover parts of this important song of triumph, so please read the whole Psalm. You'll be encouraged and blessed.

David wrote this song to Jesus, *"the Chief Musician"* (Psa. 68 subtitle NKJV). This song exalts Jesus, our Warrior King, as He goes to war on our behalf and destroys our adversaries.[1] David begins this Psalm by shouting a powerful War Cry, **"Let God arise**, *spring into action with awesome power and scatter Your enemies. Let those who hate You flee, run for their lives from Your presence"* (Psa. 68:1 KJV/NET/tPt/NLT/Har). The Hebrew word for the phrase *"let God arise"* is *kumah*, a War Cry.[2] When we shout it, the terror of God falls on the wicked one.

Here are a few reasons why demonic forces tremble when we shout *"Kumah!"* By faith, we shout this War Cry and ask the Lord to arise in our midst:

1. ***Kumah!*** God, arise and *"strike all my enemies on the jaw.* **You will shatter the teeth of the wicked, breaking the power of their words to harm me***"* (Psa. 3:7 NET/NLT/tPt).

2. ***Kumah!*** God, arise and *"manifest the power of Your hand.* **Break the arm of the wicked,** *and all their strong-arm tactics"* (Psa. 10:12, 15 Har/KJV/tPt/NLT).

3. ***Kumah!*** God, arise against our *"deadly enemies ... like lions eager to tear [us] apart ... Stand against them,* **cast them down to the ground***, and make an end of them with Your sword"* (Psa. 17:9, 12-13 KJV/tPt/NLT/NEB).

Glory! As we shout *"Kumah!"* God responds to our War Cry. He breaks the jaw of the wicked. God breaks the power of the enemy's words to harm us because now, all the evil one can do is mumble. With His mighty hand, God breaks the arms of the enemy. The devil can no longer strike us with shame and worthlessness. God knocks our adversary to the ground. He's prepared the way for us to tread on the devil's head (Luke 10:19-20). David knows how to begin a War Psalm! So shout, *"Kumah!"* our War Cry and see God's victory.

DANCE A WAR DANCE AS YOU SING THIS WAR PSALM

David is just getting warmed up. Bursting with joy, he revels in God's power and exclaims, *"As **smoke is blown away by the wind**, may You drive them away; **as wax melts when near the fire, so let the wicked perish at the presence of God**. But the godly are happy; when the righteous see God in action they'll laugh. **They rejoice, jump for joy (i.e. 'alats) before God; Yes, they rejoice (i.e., suws) exceedingly full of joy"* (Psa. 68:2-3 NIV/NASB/JB/NLT/MSG/NKJV/EXE/BBE). David gives two examples of how weak the wicked are before God. They're like smoke blown away by the wind of God's Spirit and like wax that melts before the fire of God's presence.

David tells us to rejoice as the *smoke is driven away,* and *the wax is melting.* He uses two different Hebrew words for rejoice. The first is *'alats* and the second is *suws.* We'll study both and discover how we're to rejoice in God's victory over the wicked one.

The first word *'alats* (pronounced aw-lats) means "to be joyful, rejoice, exult, to raise your hands and jump for joy."[3] When David says to rejoice, he's telling us to jump for joy! When we are overcome with God's joy, we can't just stand there. Our physical body responds to the joy of the Lord. We manifest our rejoicing in God's defeat of the evil one by jumping up and down. It's time to dance God's War Dance called the "Holy Ghost Hop and Stomp!"

King Solomon used the word *'alats* in Proverbs concerning those who love God. *"When **the righteous rejoice, jump for joy (i.e. 'alats)**, there is great glory. The triumphant joy of God's lovers **releases great glory**"* (Prov. 28:12a NKJV/ERRB/tPt). Lovers of God rejoice by jumping with triumphant joy and releasing God's great glory. But we don't stop there.

The second Hebrew word for rejoice is *suws* (pronounced soos or cease) and means "to be bright, to exult, be glad, to rejoice by leaping and springing, to turn around in joy and dance around in circles."[4] David says to express our rejoicing through specific physical actions like jumping, leaping, springing about, and dancing in circles.[5] We're going to need plenty of room as we jump, leap, and spring all over the place!

OUR REJOICING BUILDS A ROAD FOR THE RIDER OF THE CLOUDS!

In his introduction to Psalm 68, David exhorts us to shout *"Kumah!"* a War Cry, to dance God's War Dance of jumping, leaping, and springing, and to sing this War Psalm. David said, *"Sing to God! Sing praises [and] play music to His name. Lift up a song for Him [and]* **make a highway for the Cloud–Rider, build a road for the Rider of the Clouds, Whose name is Yah!** *And rejoice, jump for joy (i.e. 'alats) before Him"* (Psa. 68:4 NASB/JB/DeW/MSG/tPt/ERRB).

Dancing God's War Dance creates a Highway in the sky for the Cloud–Rider.

As we shout our War Cry, sing this War Psalm, and dance our War Dance, we create a road—a highway in the sky for *"the Cloud–Rider"* to appear! Enthroned on our praises (Psa. 22:3 KJV), the Lord arrives riding His cloud of glory.

When the *Cloud–Rider* appears and His glory falls, we rejoice! We sing with David that the Lord is the *"Father to the fatherless, Defender of widows, God sets the lonely in families, in a permanent home, He sets the prisoners free and leads them into prosperity"* (Psa. 68:5-6 KJV/DeW/JB/NIV/NLT). Seeing God's heart of love for those in need sets our hearts to dancing!

GOD'S ARMY OF WOMEN–WARRIORS

The Lord's purpose behind all this rejoicing—shouting a War Cry, singing this War Psalm, and dancing a War Dance—is for the Cloud–Rider to come and lead us into war! David exclaims, *"O Lord, it was You Who* **led Your people into battle, when You marched** *through the desert"* (Psa. 68:7 tPt/NET). When our praise and worship move into *high praise and warfare-worship,* it means God's warriors, like the warriors of Israel, are ready for the Lord to lead us into battle. We lift up our *"two-edged sword"* of God's Word (Psa. 149:6 KJV) and wait for the marching orders from our Warrior–King.

We don't have to wait long. *"The Lord gives the command, the battle cry, the Word of the gospel with power,* **and great is the army of warring women of Zion who cry out** *the happy news"* (Psa. 68:11 RSV/tPt/Har/TLB/NET with footnote). God's got an Army, and it includes women. God's marching orders specifically involve His great Army of warring women to attack. They charge shouting their battle cry—the Word of the Gospel!

God's women warriors attack as they cry out the happy news with power. They rejoice, *"The kings of armies that came to destroy us have fled! Now all the women of Israel are dividing the spoils"* (Psa. 68:12 KJV/TLB/tPt). In this battle, the *kings of armies* represent demonic forces trying to destroy people. Big mistake, you don't mess with the mothers of Israel; those ladies are she-bears! The enemy must flee from them and the power of God's gospel. The *spoils* represent the people who accept God's good news, are saved, and brought into God's home.

JESUS IS OUR RESURRECTED WARRIOR–KING

Psalm 68 is a War Psalm about the ultimate battle Jesus fought and won for all of God's creation. David begins this song with the War Cry, *"Let God arise!"* (Psa. 68:1 KJV), and later tells what God did as He arose. *"When You ascended on high, You led a crowd of captives, leading them in triumphal procession. And gifts were given to men, even the once rebellious, so that they may dwell with the Lord God"* (Psa. 68:18 NIV/NLT/tPt). Paul says this is when Jesus rose from the dead (Eph. 4:8-9). The Lord has opened David's eyes. He looks into the future and sees Jesus, the Son of God, ascend into heaven and reveals to David that one day we'll dwell with the Lord there.

Paul explains that in order for Jesus to ascend, it *"means He first descended into hell"* (Eph. 4:9 NLT/tPt). As the spotless Lamb of God Jesus was worthy, death could not hold Him. Jesus arose from the grave. He had defeated sin, death, hell, and the devil *"so that His rule might now fill the entire universe"* (Eph. 4:10 NLT). The Warrior–King in Psalm 68 is Jesus, our Resurrected King who leads us into battle. When Jesus leads the attack, we always experience victory.

Jesus has fought and won. He gives out the spoils of His victory. Paul reveals the gifts Jesus gives are the five-fold ministries of *"apostles, prophets, evangelists, pastors, and teachers"* (Eph. 4:11 KJV). These leadership gifts equip us and perfect us until we are mature warriors of God (Eph. 4:12-13).

No longer *"children, forever changing our minds about what to believe because someone has told us something different or because someone has cleverly lied to us and made the lie sound like the truth"* (Eph. 4:14 NLT). It's time to grow up! The Lord does not call children to go to war–God calls adults.

> It's time to grow up. Children do not go to war—adults do.

BEFORE GOING TO WAR, WE GET IN GOD'S BATTLE FORMATION

Our nation is in desperate straits. It's time to go to war, but before God leads us into battle, He must place His warriors in the correct battle formation. In every battle, when Israel followed the Lord's battle plan, they won. When the Holy Spirit directs David to attack the enemy, He gives him instructions on how to assemble and line up his army for the battle.

David exclaims, *"God, everyone can see **Your victory parade-the victory march of my God and King** into His holy place! The singers marching in front, the players on instruments last, between them are young women playing tambourines"* (Psa. 68:24-25 ERV/NRSV/NKJV/NLT/JB). The singers like Judah, the tribe of praisers, led the charge in the past (Judg. 1:1-2). Next, are God's women warriors beating their hand drums (tambourines)—a vital weapon in God's Army. They knew the Lord beat the enemy in rhythm with their tambourines (Isa. 30:32). Bringing up the rear are God's musical warriors playing their musical weapons. They're releasing the power of God through the supernatural sound waves of their weapons of music.

The Holy Spirit may direct you to march around your church property and claim the land for God. Better yet, march around your town square, city hall, and courthouse and claim your city for God! But you only do this *if you know* the Lord is directing you to do it. It is wise to get confirmation from other spiritual leaders before engaging in this level of warfare. *"Don't go to war without wise guidance and the right strategy. In the abundance of many advisors there is victory"* (Prov. 24:6 NLT/NET/NASB/GW). We attack when and how God says to attack!

David said, *"This God of ours is a God Who saves us over and over. The Sovereign LORD rescues us from death many times.* **God will smash the heads of His enemies, shattering their strength.** *He will make heads roll, split the skulls of those who still love their evil ways as He marched out of heaven"* (Psa. 68:20 JB/NLT/MSG/tPt/BBE). This graphic image reveals what God does to the wicked one in the spiritual realm. To people who hold onto their evil ways, God attacks the stronghold of their minds by splitting their skulls (symbolically) with the Truth. Then God can set them free of the lies and deceptions holding them in captivity.

After God crushes the heads of our demonic enemies, what do we do? God says, *"My people will be the conquerors. Their feet will wade in the blood of their enemies.* **They will soon have you under their feet! They will crush you until there is nothing left!"** (Psa. 68:23 tPt/Jub/ HCSB). As the Lord fights through us, the promise of Jesus is fulfilled, *"I saw satan fall like lightning from heaven. Behold,* **I have given you authority to trample on and crush snakes and scorpions, and over all the power of the enemy, and nothing will harm you"** (Luke 10:18-19 NIV/NASB). It's wonderful when we walk in Jesus' power, but our greatest joy is knowing our names are written in heaven (Luke 10:20). Authority over the devil is just a side benefit.

> *Our greatest joy is that we are saved.*
> *Power over the devil is just a side benefit.*

Use this War Psalm as a Word-Sword to resist the devil. Dance as you *"make music for the One Who strides the ancient skies. There He is, Sky-Rider! Listen to His thunderous voice of might split open the heavens. Proclaim His majesty for His glory shines down on Israel. His mighty strength soars* **in the clouds of glory"** (Psa. 68:33-34 tPt/MSG). Our warfare-worship opens the way for the *Cloud–Rider, the Sky-Rider,* to come in glory. This is the way we fight. We follow Him as He leads us into battle.

Jesus leads us into battle. We shout, **"Sound Your battle cry against the wild beast of the reeds.** *You are awesome, O God, as You emerge from Your holy temple.* **As Your glory streams from Your Holy Place, the God of power shares His mighty strength with Israel and all His people**. *God, we give our highest praise to You"* (Psa. 68:30, 35 NIV/NET/tPt). The Lord attacks, shouting His battle cry. His glory falls upon us, and He shares His mighty strength with all His warriors! Covered in His glory, we follow the God of power into victory!

PSALM 96—THE LORD REIGNS

The word *'alats* is also used when David brought the Ark of the Covenant into Jerusalem (1 Chron. 16:1). David instructs Asaph to lead the people in praise and worship. Asaph exhorts them, *"Let the heavens be glad, and let the earth rejoice, twirl (i.e., giyl). Say among the nations, '***The LORD reigns***.' Let the sea roar, and everything in it shout!* **Let the fields rejoice,** *jump for joy (i.e. 'alats) and all that is in it"* (1 Chron. 16:31-32 NKJV/NET/ERRB). The sea roars, and the fields jump for joy.

These verses are also found in Psalm 96, a song of praise to the *"King of the World"* (tPt subtitle). The psalmist says, *"The LORD reigns! ... Let the heavens rejoice, and **let the earth be glad, twirl (i.e., giyl)! Let the sea roar (i.e., ra'am)** and all that is in it shout! **Let the fields jump for joy (i.e. 'alats)** and all that is in it. Then all **the trees of the forest will shout with joy (i.e., ranan)**"* (Psa. 96:10-12 NKJV/NET/ERRB/NIV). The heavens rejoice, the seas roar, the earth dances (*giyl*), the trees shout, and the fields jump for joy for the Lord our God reigns as King of the universe. With all this going on, we're going to feel really awkward if we don't join the rest of the universe in their celebration and dance to the Lord, the King of glory!

In this Psalm, there's a lot of rejoicing going on militarily. The earth is dancing in circles, the *giyl* War Dance. The sea is roaring *"Ra'am,"* the War Cry of God's thunder. The trees of the forest are shouting *"Ranan,"* the War Cry of God's overcomers, and the fields are jumping for joy.[6] Like Psalm 68, Psalm 96 is a War Psalm to sing of God's victory over His enemies.

God is triumphant: *"For the Lord is great and greatly to be praised; He is to be feared above all gods. **For all the gods of the nations are false gods, worthless idols**"* (Psa. 96:4-5 NKJV/NIV/BBE/NET). The Septuagint says it best *"**all the gods of the nations are demons**"* (NETS). This Psalm is full of military terminology because God has defeated all the false gods—worthless idols, the demons of this land.

The Lord reigns. Join all creation in celebrating God's victory over the evil one. Singing War Songs and dancing War Dances is the perfect way to rejoice in His triumph!

ENDNOTES

1. Footnotes to Psalm 68:1 in the NET Bible and Nelson Study Bible.
2. For more information concerning our War Cry, Kumah, see Book Three in "God's Heart of War Series" entitled *The War Cries of God*, pp. 255-279.
3. The Hebrew word *'alats* is Strong's H5970 at: Benner, page 404 and http://www.blbclassic.org/lang/lexicon/lexicon.cfm?Strongs=H5970&t=KJV.
4. The Hebrew word *suws* is Strong's H7797 at: http://www.blbclassic.org/lang/lexicon/lexicon.cfm?Strongs=H7797&t=KJV.
5. Here's the difference between leap, jump, and spring. *Leap* refers to the distance, how far we go horizontally. *Jump* is how high we go vertically. *Spring* refers to the speed, how fast we go.
6. For more information concerning our War Cries, *Ra'am* and *Ranan*, see Book Three in "God's Heart of War Series" entitled *The War Cries of God*, pp. 203-227 and 129-156.

CHAPTER SIX

WAR DANCES BIND THE ENEMY WITH GOD'S CHAINS

*Let them praise His name in the dance ... **To bind their kings with chains,** and their nobles with fetters of iron.*

Psa. 149:3a, 8 NKJV

GOD TURNS OUR MOURNING INTO DANCING

The next War Dance we're going to study is also found in the Psalms. It is first used in Psalm 30, a song by David entitled *He Healed Me* (tPt subtitle). He wrote it for the dedication of the Temple and a celebration of God's victory. David rejoices, "[F]or You have rescued me. **You refused to let my enemies triumph over me.** I cried out for a miracle and You healed me! You brought me back from the brink of death ... Now *here I am, alive and well, fully restored"* (Psa. 30:1-3 NLT/tPt). David experienced God's deliverance, protection, healing, and restoration.

David asked the Lord, "[B]e gracious to me, O LORD, **show me Your favor**" (Psa. 30:10a NASB/Rhm). When God's favor and grace touch us, He turns our ***"mourning into a joyful, whirling, round dance (i.e., machowl) of ecstatic praise!** You have taken away my sackcloth of sad heaviness and wrapped me in the glory-garments of praise, gladness, and joy"* (Psa. 30:11 NIV/NLT/ERRB/tPt/WYC). God is never depressed. God is joy personified, and the joy of the Lord is contagious. When we draw near to Him, depression and sadness must flee. God's favor surrounds us, and His joy is wrapped around us like a garment. Bursting with joy, we can't stand still. Our mourning is turned into a dance of ecstatic praise!

Everything we do for the Lord, we are to do with all our might, and that includes dancing unto Him. The Hebrew word for dancing in this song is *machowl* (pronounced maw-hole) and means "to spin around from joy or pain, to dance a (round) dance."[1] Visit a Jewish wedding, and you'll see an example of a circle (round) dance. They dance the Hora (or Horah), where the dancers link hands or put their arms over each other's shoulders to create a circle around the bride and groom. They'll dance for hours. You'll quickly realize Jewish people love to dance!

This image of *encircling* someone as we dance is revealed in the word picture definition of *machowl*. Its Hebrew letters *mem, chet, vav,* and *lamed* can literally mean "to be surrounded and protected by the mighty power of the Shepherd and His Rod."[2] If we're not careful, we can miss the impact of this definition about the Shepherd and His Rod. They're mentioned in Psalm Two when God tells His Son, *"Your domain will stretch to the ends of the earth. And **You will***

shepherd them with unlimited authority, crushing their rebellion with a rod of iron, *and will dash them to pieces like pottery"* (Psa. 2:8-9 tPt/NIV). In this psalm, God warns the wicked about His Shepherd and tells us of His unlimited authority and rebellion-crushing Rod.

When we realize we're surrounded and protected by our Great Shepherd, we will dance the *machowl* because dancing in a circle like this reflects the revelation of being *surrounded, encircled* by the power of our Shepherd and His Rod!

Our round dance is a prophetic picture of God surrounding us like a wall with His power, but this dance is more than just a symbol. As we dance to the Lord, it creates things in the Spirit. Our round dance forms a literal *spiritual wall of protection* around those we dance.

> A round dance creates a spiritual wall of protection.

The *machowl* is the perfect dance for newlyweds who are starting their life together. As family, relatives, and friends dance around them, it's a prophetic picture of God blessing their marriage with His wall of protection. It's not just prophetic; *it's a physical manifestation* of God's wall of protection around the newlyweds, created by the Lord for their protection. Whether the dancers know it or not, God's purpose is to use them as His wall to stand around and protect this couple as they start their new covenant walk together.

The Machowl Circular Dance is a War Dance

The *machowl* round dance is also a powerful War Dance. *Machowl* is derived from the root word *chuwl,* which refers to two physical actions: "to whirl in motion or to writhe in pain."³ *Chuwl* can also mean "to dance in a circle, to twist, to turn around, and whirl (in a circular or spiral manner)" or "to writhe in pain from a wound or the *labor* pains of childbirth."⁴ *Chuwl* creates an image of wild physical motions and refers to *the battle* waged to bring new life, both physical and spiritual, into the world. So, *machowl* is a War Dance of *"whirling for joy"* in victory and a War Dance of *"writhing in labor pains"* in childbirth. Both are dances reflecting strong emotions as the result of a struggle.

The root word *chuwl* gives us more revelation concerning God's *Machowl* War Dance. Along with *machowl*, there are two more Hebrew words derived from *chuwl*. The first is *cheyl*, which refers to "an army, a wall, fortress, fortification, or rampart."⁵ The second is *chayil* which refers to "strength, power, and might for war (i.e.. soldiers, men of valor)."⁶ Do not get confused with these words and their definitions because these four words are connected. Through them, God shows us that in His Kingdom, a *wall or fortress and an army of strong warriors* are created by His War Dance of *dancing in a circle!*

> In God's Kingdom, dancing in circles creates strong walls and strong warriors.

Everything we do for the Lord, we do by faith. We dance by faith, and as we dance this circular dance, we create a wall, a fortress of protection in the spiritual realm. We become the strong warriors in God's army, the *"living stones"* (1 Pet. 2:5) who make up this wall.

As we dance, God builds His Holy Ghost stronghold, His mighty citadel that repels every demonic attack. Our round dance is not just for weddings; it's for war. At a wedding, we form a wall and *face inwards* towards the couple to bless them. In a battle, we still stay in a circle, but we form a wall and *face outwards* to resist any assault and protect those in the center.

This War Dance Binds the Enemy with God's Chains!

Machowl next appears in Psalm 149. But before we study that, we will first look more closely at Psalm 2 because it lays the foundation to understand Psalm 149 better.

Psalm 2 is a War Psalm and gives the purpose for all the Psalms of war. The Psalmist asks, **"Why do the nations rebel, conspire, [and] rage?** *Why do the peoples plot a vain thing?* **The kings of the earth rise up in revolt [and] prepare for battle;** *the rulers plot together against the LORD and against His Anointed One. They say,* **'Let us break Their chains** *They've put on us. Let's free ourselves,* **and cast off Their fetters'"** (Psa. 2:1-3 NET/NIV/KJV/NAB/JB/NLT). A battle continues to rage between the kingdoms of this world. The kings and rulers on earth are rising up against the Lord and His Anointed One.

The Anointed One is Jesus, God's Son, and the chains and fetters the rebellious want to break and throw off are God's Word. *The ungodly see God's Word as restrictive chains*. They want to do whatever they desire to do. They want to boast, "I did it my way," not God's way.

They don't realize they're already in bondage. The ungodly are chained by a spirit of lawlessness (2 Thess. 2:1-17). The so-called freedom they desire is a false freedom. They want *to be free* to steal, lie, covet, commit adultery, and even kill (Ex. 20:13-17). They have no desire to walk in God's love on His *"highway of holiness"* (Isa. 35:8 NASB), and the result is chaos on earth!

In the face of this rage and rebellion, God laughs because He has set His Son as King (Psa. 2:4, 6-9) and has a plan. Jesus is King and has a kingdom of warriors, and the Father has a mission for these warriors to fulfill.

God reveals their mission throughout the Psalms and comes to His glorious conclusion in Psalm 149. As God's warriors come into His presence, they *"sing to the Lord a new song ...* **they delight, twirl (i.e., giyl) in their King** *... they praise His name* **with dancing the round dance (i.e., machowl)!** *They sing praises to Him with the tambourine and harp"* (Psa. 149:1-3 NET/NASB/ERRB). As God's warriors, we sing a new song, twirl in delight, dance a round dance, and play our tambourines and harps to exalt our King. After we're finished, we stand at attention before our Commander in battle formation with *"the high praises of God in [our] mouth and a two-edged sword in [our] hands,* **for [our] shouted praises are [our] weapons of war!"** (Psa. 149:6 NASB/tPt). We wait for His orders to send us into battle.

We don't have to wait long. The Lord of Hosts declares, *"These warring weapons will bring vengeance on every opposing force and every resistant power ..."***to bind their kings in chains, and their nobles with fetters of iron.** *Praise-filled warriors will execute the judgment-doom written against their enemies"* (Psa. 149:7-9a tPt/NASB/NIV/NET). God orders us to put His chains and fetters back on the kings and nobles. These leaders represent the *opposing forces and resistant powers* in both the physical and spiritual realm set against God and His kingdom. In the past, they resisted God's rule and cast off His chains (Psa. 2:2-3), but the tables are turned. God, through our praise and worship, now binds and opposes them!

The decree of our Commander is to bind these rebellious forces. To obey His command is *"an honor and glory He gives to all His godly lovers. Praise the LORD!"* (Psa. 149:9b NASB/ NLT/KJV/tPt). God has given us the honor of binding spiritual forces with His chains and bringing people to repentance, and seeing them restored back to God.

We are warned in Psalm 2, *"[L]earn our lesson before it's too late. Submit to correction. Serve the Lord with fear! Repent in terror!* **Kiss the Son, lest He be angry**" (Psa. 2:10-11 tPt/ NET/ NKJV). For *"many blessings are waiting for all who put their trust in Him"* (Psa. 2:12 tPt/ NKJV). The conclusion of this song is the Father desires to bless all who trust Him.

> God gives us the honor to bind rebellious spirits with His chains.

Psalm 149 tells how we put God's chains on rebellious spirits. It gives us the spiritual weapons we'll need. We bind this demonic force with our warfare worship of high praises, musical weapons, dancing, and the Sword of God's Word. The specific War Dance is *machowl* because it's the dance where we encircle something or someone. It's a *dance of love,* as we encircle people and protect them with God's protection. It's *a dance of war* as we encircle the enemy's stronghold, destroy it, and bring God's deliverance to those who were bound.

We see this principle of encircling a stronghold and destroying it in the battle of Jericho. On the seventh day, the Israelites *marched around the city* seven times. They formed a wall of warriors that surrounded the city. When they sounded the Shofar and shouted the War Cry, the walls of Jericho fell (Josh. 6:20). All these acts and sounds of faith combined to become the Rod of the Shepherd that pushed over the walls of Jericho.

Another example of God's circular dance surrounding the enemy's camp is when the king of Aram sends an army to capture Elisha. The next morning his servant saw an *"army with horses and chariots **surrounding the city**"* and cried out, *"Oh no, my lord! What shall we do?"* Elisha calmly replied, *"Don't be afraid. Those who are with us are more than those who are with them"* (2 Kings 6:15-16 NIV). Elisha's servant was freaking out—they were surrounded by the enemy, but Elisha was undisturbed. His servant realized Elisha had lost his mind, that nobody was out there except a huge, hostile army, and he thought, *We're all going to die!*

But then Elisha prays to God, *"'[O]pen his eyes that he may see.' And the Lord opened his servant's eyes, and when he looked up, he saw the hillside full of horses and chariots of fire **all around Elisha**. The whole mountainside [was] full of horses and chariots of fire **surrounding Elisha!**"* (2 Kings 6:17 NIV/NLT/MSG). O Lord, we cry, "Open our eyes!"

Often in the natural realm, it seems like the adversary has surrounded us, but in reality, the enemy's camp is surrounded by God's heavenly army of angels! Lord, put this revelation deep in our spirit, so we're strong like Elisha. Show us that more are with us than are with the enemy. We're surrounded and protected by Your angel army. Let us see them dancing in circles around us.

OUR ROUND DANCE AND GOD'S NEW COVENANT

Machowl is also mentioned in one of the most powerful prophecies in the Old Testament. It's the prophecy about God's *"new covenant"* that He will make with the children of Israel and Judah (Jer. 31:31 with Matt. 26:28). The Lord gave this promise to Israel when they were enslaved to the Babylonians, and it still produces joy and wonder as we read it today.

In Israel's time of distress, the Lord gave them this beautiful promise, *"I have loved you with an everlasting love. With unfailing loving-kindness, I have drawn you to Myself. I will build you again, and you, Virgin Israel, will be rebuilt.* **Again, you will take up your tambourines and go out to dance the round dance (i.e., machowl) with the joyful"** (Jer.31:3-4 NIV/NLT/ERRB). What great news for Israel! God loves them and is going to restore their homeland!

Like a shepherd, God will gather His scattered flock and bring them home (Jer. 31:10). *"The people will come home and climb up Zion's slopes shouting with joy, their faces beaming because of God's bounty ...* **Then the virgin will dance the round dance (i.e., machowl) for joy**, *and the men—old and young—will join in the celebration"* (Jer. 31:12-13 NLT/MSG/ERRB). God is setting the stage for His grand announcement, *"'Behold, the days are coming,' declares the LORD, 'when* **I will make a new covenant** *with the house of Israel and with the house of Judah'"* (Jer. 31:31 NASB). God says, *"This is the brand-new covenant that I will make with Israel when the time comes. I will put My law within them—***write it on their hearts!***—and be their God. And they will be My people"* (Jer. 31:33 MSG). God will write His law not on tablets of stone but on the tablets of their heart. What a perfect prophetic picture of God's new covenant.

As he introduced God's great news to Israel (Jer. 31:1-14), the Holy Spirit inspired Jeremiah to mention dancing—the *machowl* round dance—because God's new covenant means *new life is being birthed* in the Spirit. We learned earlier that our circular War Dance also refers to *"writhing in labor pains."* The *machowl* is the exact dance needed as new life is being born.

We could dance our *machowl* round dance while babies are being born because this is a dance of war, and birthing babies is a battle. Just ask any mother! If you've visited the Labor and Delivery unit at a hospital, all that screaming, shouting, and crying make it sound like a war zone as mothers are fighting with all their might to see their child brought into this world.

It's the same during times of revival when the Holy Ghost is pouring out God's Spirit of conviction and His gift of repentance. There is a lot of weeping and crying out to the Father for His mercy and forgiveness. It is a battleground, and the gates of hell are falling as people break out and enter God's kingdom.

> Birthing babies is a battle. Both to be born and be born again happen in War Zones.

We will rejoice as new warriors join God's Army! We will dance and shout, "O Lord, protect this new warrior. Make them strong—Army of God strong!"

Let Everything That Moves Dance Unto The Lord

We end this chapter with one more verse about *machowl*, our round dance. It's found in Psalm 150. As the last song in the book of praise, this psalm concludes with a resounding command for everything that has breath to praise the Lord. As we sing this psalm, we can feel the Spirit rising within us in ever-increasing waves of praise and awe.

Read Psalm 150 out loud; better yet, sing it. It speaks for itself. I'll only say one thing: of all the Hebrew words for dance used in the Old Testament, the Holy Spirit inspired the writers of the Psalms to use *machowl*—our round War Dance—as the specific dance God calls us to dance in the last two Psalms (Psa. 149:3 and 150:4). He's telling us this is a very important War Dance.

The Hallelujah Chorus

Praise the LORD! Praise God in His sanctuary!
Praise Him in His stronghold in the sky!
Praise Him for His mighty acts of power;
Praise Him according to His excellent greatness!
Praise Him with Shofars blasting!
Praise Him with piano and guitar!
Praise Him with drums and dancing (i.e., machowl)!
Praise Him with stringed instruments and flute!
Praise Him with the loud, resounding clash of cymbals!
Praise Him with every instrument you can find!
Let everything that has breath praise the Lord!
Let everyone everywhere join in the crescendo of ecstatic praise to Yahweh! Praise the LORD!

Psalm 150 NLT/tPt/NIV/NKJV/CJB/NASB

ENDNOTES

1. The Hebrew word *machowl* is Strong's H4234 at Benner, p. 271 and at: http://www.blbclassic.org/lang/lexicon/lexicon.cfm?Strongs=H4234&t=KJV,
2. Seekins, pp. 10-11.
3. Baker, Warren and Carpenter, Eugene. "The Complete Word Study Dictionary: Old Testament." AMG Publishers, Chattanooga, TN, © 2003, pp. 319-320.
4. The Hebrew word *chuwl* is Strong's H2342 at: http://www.blbclassic.org/lang/lexicon/Lexicon.cfm?Strongs=H2342&t=KJV,
5. The Hebrew word *cheyl* is Strong's H2426 at: http://www.blbclassic.org/lang/lexicon/lexicon.cfm?Strongs=H2426&t=KJV,
6. The Hebrew word *chayil* is Strong's H2428 at: http://www.blbclassic.org/lang/lexicon/lexicon.cfm?strongs=H2428&t=KJV,

CHAPTER SEVEN

WE ARE TRANSFORMED INTO GOD'S STAG

He jumped up, stood on his feet, and began to walk! Then, walking, leaping, and praising God, he went into the Temple with them.

Acts 3:8 NLT

THE LAME SHALL LEAP LIKE THE MIGHTY STAG

In this chapter, we'll study some War Dances involving jumping, leaping, and skipping. The first dance is found in a prophecy by Isaiah when God will restore the wasteland like a garden. Isaiah starts with the promise, *"[T]he desert shall rejoice twirl (i.e., giyl) and blossom as the rose"* (Isa. 35:1b NKJV/ERRB). Isaiah begins this prophecy with *giyl*, a War Dance we looked at earlier, which means to spin around, go in a circle, twirl, and leap for joy.

Giyl is used in the next verse, *"Every dry and barren place will burst forth with abundant blossoms, **twirling, dancing, and spinning with delight (i.e., giyl)!"*** (Isa. 35:2 tPt/ERRB). When the desert begins to flourish, it's a sign God is pouring out His blessings. When the world sees barren places burst with life, dance, and spin with delight, they'll know it's being touched by God! *When the world sees us dancing and spinning, they'll know we're being blessed by God.*

> When the desert starts dancing, the world will know God is blessing it!

The desert dances because it hears the good news from Isaiah, *"My people will see the awesome glory of God. Look, here comes your God! **He is breaking through to give you victory ... He comes to save you!"*** (Isa. 35:2-4 tPt). God is coming in all His glory to save His people, and this is what He does: *"Then the eyes of the blind shall be opened, and the ears of the deaf shall be unstopped. Then **the lame will leap and dance (i.e., dalag) like the stag**, and those who cannot speak will shout with joy"* (Isa. 35:5-6 NKJV/GNT/NABRE). These are all signs the gospel of the kingdom is being preached: blind eyes see, deaf ears hear, the lame leap and dance like the stag, and mute tongues shout (Matt. 11:4-5). Jesus, the Son of God, has come to save His people. Like this desert in Isaiah, we were once barren, but now Jesus makes us flourish and blossom like a rose. We join the desert in its dance as we leap like a wild stag in the victory!

The Hebrew word for leap is *dalag* (pronounced daw-lag) and means "to leap or jump over, and spring."[1] Its Hebrew letters: *dalet, lamed,* and *gimel* can literally mean when we leap; we are "walking through the door onto the pathway into the authority of the Shepherd and His Rod."[2] Don't skip over the power in this phrase, "the authority of the Shepherd and His Rod." Recall in Psalm 2 that the Lord had established His Son as King and said, *"You will shepherd them with a rod of iron, crushing their rebellion as an iron rod smashes jars of clay"* (Psa. 2:8-9 NKJV/tPt). God's Shepherd has a Rod, and it's powerful. Jesus uses it to smash rebellion. As we leap in this War Dance, we jump right through the door onto the pathway that brings us to the Shepherd and His Rod of power.

David knew the power and anointing of this leaping War Dance. He declared, *"With You I can charge into battle, I can run through a troop and defeat a battalion.* ***With my God I can leap (i.e., dalag) over a wall and overcome their defenses****. I can crush an enemy horde [and] advance through every stronghold that stands in front of me"* (Psa. 18:29 CEB/KJV/JUB/tPt). This is an image "of a divinely empowered warrior charging against an army in almost superhuman fashion [and] emphasizes his God-given military superiority" (Psa. 18:29 NET footnote). Anointed with God's power, David is victorious. He can leap over every stronghold standing in his way!

David could do this because *"**It is God Who gives me strength; He removes the obstacles in my way***. He makes my feet like hind's feet, and sets me upon my high place"* (Psa. 18:32-33 NIV/NASB/ NET). We pray, "God, give us Your strength. Remove the obstacles. Anoint us like You anointed David and make us Your mighty Stag." If a demonic stronghold is in our way, it's no problem. We attack it by dancing like David, and like a stag, we leap over it.

Another example of leaping like a stag is found with our Bridegroom. The Beloved cries out, *"Listen! My Lover is approaching! Look!* ***Here He comes leaping (i.e., dalag) with joy over the mountains****, skipping in love over the hills that* *separate us, to come to me. My Lover is like a gazelle, graceful; **like a young stag**"* (SoS. 2:8-9a NET/MSG/tPt). David leaps over walls; our Bridegroom leaps over mountains and skips over hills! These high places represent kingdoms of this world that stand against the Lord and us. They're not an obstacle for our Bridegroom. Like a young stag, He leaps right over them to get to us. Let's join our Bridegroom in this leaping War Dance and as God's anointed Stag overcome every stronghold.

> David leaped over walls. Our Bridegroom leaps over mountains!

God said we'd leap like a stag. We looked at this promise earlier when Isaiah said, *"Then the eyes of the blind shall be opened, and the ears of the deaf shall be unstopped. Then **the lame will leap and dance (i.e., dalag) like the stag**, and those who cannot speak will shout with joy"* (Isa. 35:5-6 NKJV/GNT/NABRE). All these signs reveal God's kingdom has come (Luke 7:18-30). Jesus moves by His power when the good news is preached,

Peter knew when the gospel was preached; Jesus and His kingdom would come, and one of the signs would be that the lame would walk. So, when Peter and John met the man who was lame from birth at the Temple, Peter said to him, *"Silver and gold I do not have, but what I do have I give to you: **In the name of Jesus Christ of Nazareth, rise up and walk**. Then Peter took him by the right hand and lifted him up, and immediately his feet and ankle bones were healed and became strong. **He jumped up**, stood on his feet, and began to walk! Then, **walking, leaping, and praising God**, he went into the Temple with them. And all the people **saw him jumping up and down** and praising God"* (Acts 3:6-9 NKJV/NLT/BBE/tPt).[3] When Jesus' power is released, people praise God as they leap, jump, and dance!

Jumping, leaping, and skipping are powerful War Dances of victory, especially if you've been lame since birth! It's possible something beautiful happened here. The Greek word for lame is *cholos* (pronounced ho-los) and refers to someone who's "lame, crippled, or missing a foot."[4] Though not recorded, it is possible that this man could have been missing one or both feet, and Jesus healed him by growing out his feet. If this was the case, no wonder the people were astounded and dumbfounded (Acts 3:10-11)! For forty years, when they came to the Temple, the people had seen this man lying there lame, possibly without any feet. Now he was walking, leaping, and praising God—a miraculous sign indeed!

Going back to Isaiah's prophecy (Isa. 35:6), the Hebrew word he used for "to be lame" is *picceach* (pronounced pis-say-ah).[5] The letter-by-letter definition of *picceach* will cause us to leap for joy like this man. The Hebrew letters in *picceach* are *pey, samech,* and *chet.* They can literally mean "to be surrounded by the words spoken by the snake."[6] This man who was lame is a reflection of all of us before we met Jesus. Before Jesus saved us, we were surrounded by the lies of the serpent. *Listening to the lies of the wicked one crippled our life-walk.* With lame feet, we were unable to tread on the devil's head. We needed help.

But when we hear God's Truth, *"In the name of Jesus of Nazareth rise up and walk,"* it disperses the lies of the snake. By the power of Jesus, we not only walk; we leap, dance, and jump like a stag! The correct word to use is stag, not deer because we're not talking about a sweet little image of the cartoon, Bambi. The Hebrew word translated deer is *'ayal* and refers to a "stag, a great ram, or large she-

> Before Jesus saved us, we were all lame in our spiritual walk.

goat."⁷ The Lord makes us a great ram, His mighty stag with strong feet.

GOD'S MIGHTY STAG IS CREATED FOR BATTLE

We decree with Habakkuk and say, *"The Lord God is my strength; He makes my feet like hind's feet.* **He makes me tread on my high places [of trouble].** *He will cause me to be victorious in my instruments of music and song. Upon the necks of my enemies He causes me to mount"* (Hab. 3:19 NASB/ESV/Amp/JUB/NETS). Our War Dance of jumping does more than *express* our victory in Jesus. This leaping, stag-creating War Dance *releases* His victory.

Remember, the word for leap is *dalag* and literally means when we *leap*; we're walking through the door into the authority of the Shepherd. As we leap in this War Dance, we jump right through the door into the Shepherd's authority. We jump out of our bad situations and places of oppression right into God's atmosphere of joy and glory. If assaulted by a spirit of depression, we can counter it with a dance. We can leap out of that fog of heaviness and jump right into God's presence. With our feet empowered by His authority, we dance over that oppression.

Transformed into God's stag, we trample over every demonic *"principality and power ...* **in high places**" standing against us (Eph. 6:12 KJV). God made our feet for dancing, leaping, and treading. Jesus gives us authority *"to tread on snakes and scorpions and to overcome all the power of the enemy"* (Luke 10:19 NET/NIV). God crushes the adversary under our feet (Rom. 16:20). Leaping, jumping, and skipping manifest Jesus' triumph over the evil one and his lies. In this War

Dance, we *leap over the wall* of the devil's lies that once surrounded us and made us lame as we *jump through the door right into the power of God*!

> *In this War Dance, we leap over the wall of the devil's lies and jump right into the power of God!*

David wrote Psalm 18 when the Lord delivered him *"from the hand of all his enemies and from the paw of Saul"* (Psa. 18 subtitle NIV/tPt with footnote). This psalm is about the victory God gave to David. May we apply it to our lives and see God deliver us from all our enemies. David said God had given him power and the feet of a stag (Psa. 18:32-33). **"You've trained my hands for battle with the weapons of warfare-worship**; *now I descend into battle with power* **to chase and conquer my foes**. *You empower me for victory with Your wrap-around presence. Your power within me makes me strong to subdue ... You've set me free from captivity, and* **my feet do not slip**; *now I'm* **standing complete ready to fight some more**! *For You have armed me with strength for battle and defeated my enemies ...* **I crush them, stomp on them** *like mud in the streets. You gave me victory on every side"* (Psa. 18:34-43 tPt/ NIV/NET with footnote). Note all the references to David's feet: *to chase, do not slip, stand complete, to crush and stomp*. When God made David His mighty stag, the Lord armed, equipped, and made David ready for battle. "Lord, make us Your stag."

IT'S NOT A TIME TO MOURN; IT'S A TIME TO LEAP

Another Hebrew word used in the Old Testament, which we studied earlier, is *raqad,* and it also means to leap and dance. I bring it up again here because its primary meaning is "to stomp or trample the ground with the feet" and "to leap, skip about, to spring about wildly, to dance, and jump."[8]

Recall that the first time *raqad* is used was to describe David's actions as the Ark was returned to the city of Jerusalem, *"As the Ark of the Lord's covenant entered the City of David ... King David [was]* **dancing (i.e., raqad)** *and playing music"* (1 Chron. 15:29 NLT/NKJV). In other versions, *raqad* is also translated as *"jumping, leaping, whirling, and skipping about"* (NET/NASB/ NKJV/ NLT). David was having a good time. He was dancing into God's destiny!

Remember that the literal meaning of *raqad* was as we dance, we enter through "the door of the destiny of the Most High."[9] When we dance, we leap like David into God's destiny for us.

The word *raqad* is also used in Psalm 29, extolling the Lord's powerful voice of thunder. God's thunderous voice makes **"Lebanon dance, skip (i.e., raqad) like a calf** *and Sirion to jump, leap like a young wild ox. The voice of God's thunder* **flashes forth flames of fire** *... And* **in His Temple** *everyone shouts, 'Glory!'"* (Psa. 29:6-7, 9 NASB/MSG/ERRB/NRSV/NLT/WYC). When God thunders, things happen—nations dance, leap, jump, and skip like calves, fire flashes, and everyone shouts, "Glory!"

David concludes this song on God as King and His promise to His people, saying, *"The LORD sat enthroned at the Flood, and the LORD sits enthroned as King forever.* **The LORD will give strength, military power to His people;** *the LORD will bless His people with His kiss of peace"* (Psa. 29:10 NKJV/NRSV/ tPt/NET with footnote). The Lord sits as King for all eternity and gives His warriors military power for war. Made strong with the power of Jesus, we triumph in every battle. After the victory, we receive the King's kiss of *Shalom peace*.

Solomon says, "*For everything there is an appointed, a fixed time, a right time for every activity under heaven. A time to weep, and a time to laugh. A time to mourn and a time to dance, skip (i.e., raqad)*" (Eccl. 3:1, 4 NET/BBE/MSG/YLT). God is pouring out His Spirit all over the earth, and this is the fixed time for us to jump, leap, and skip. Now is the appointed time, the right season for us to dance. Today is the day for us to *leap out* of our problems and *jump right into* the power of God!

God is pouring out His Spirit.
Now is the appointed time to dance!

ENDNOTES

1. The Hebrew word *dalag* is Strong's H1801 at: http://www.blbclassic.org/lang/lexicon/lexicon.cfm?Strongs=H1801&t=KJV.
2. Seekins, pp. 10-11.
3. When Peter prays for this man, he is standing on God's promise. The Lord *"brought His people out with **silver and gold** and **there was none feeble** among His tribes"* (Psa. 105:37 NET/NKJV). Peter is saying, "I don't have the silver and gold but I do have God's healing power." He knew God's promise that none of His people would be feeble. The Hebrew word for feeble is *kashal* and means to be weak in the legs, especially the ankles. If the man had a choice, he would want healed feet rather than money.
4. The Greek word *cholos* is Strong's G5560 at: http://www.blbclassic.org/lang/lexicon/lexicon.cfm?Strongs=G5560&t=KJV.
5. The Hebrew word *picceach* is Strong's H6455 at: http://www.blbclassic.org/lang/lexicon/lexicon.cfm?Strongs=H6455&t=KJV.
6. Seekins, pp. 10-11.
7. The Hebrew word *'ayal* is Strong's H354 at: http://www.blbclassic.org/lang/lexicon/Lexicon.cfm?Strongs=H354&t=KJV.
8. The Hebrew word *raqad* is Strong's H7540 at: http://www.blbclassic.org/lang/lexicon/lexicon.cfm?Strongs=H7540&t=KJV.
9. Seekins, pp. 10-11.

Chapter Eight

The War Dance of God's Majestic War Horse

He laughs at fear, and is afraid of nothing ... Shaking with passion, he paws the ground. He races off at a gallop into battle when the [war] trumpet sounds.

Job 39:22; 24 NIV/BBE/NLT/MSG/Amp

God's War Horse is His Ultimate Warrior

In spiritual warfare, the Lord does not want sheep as His warriors—God needs His War Horses, specifically created for battle. A day is coming when God *"will care for My people, the nation of Judah, and **I will change this flock of sheep into charging war horses.** The Lord will **transform them into His majestic, powerful war horses for battle"** (Zech. 10:3 CEV/

CJB/GNT/ NET). We're not just the sheep of God's pasture (Psa. 100:3); in times of war, God transforms us into *"His royal war horse **for battle**"* (Zech. 10:3 ISV). God is in the transformation business! "Lord, change us from sheep into Your War Horses to extend Your Kingdom on earth."

God's War Horses are critical in attacking and defeating the anti-christ and bringing victory in the last days. God's destiny for His War Horse is to destroy Babylon, the world system of the anti-christ!

> God transforms His sheep into His War Horses to destroy the anti-christ and the kingdom of darkness.

It is not in the scope of this book to cover God's purposes for His War Horses. We will cover this in Book Six in "God's Heart of War Series," entitled *The War Horses of God*. For now, our focus is the way God's War Horses, His ultimate warriors, love to fight. Just as natural horses love to *prance*, God's supernatural War Horses love to *dance*.

GOD CREATED WAR HORSES TO DANCE

God created horses to prance and dance. Their desire to dance is found in the Hebrew word for horse. It's the word *cuwc*, which refers "to a horse leaping" or "to the swift and cheerful flight of a swallow." It comes from a root word that means "to skip for joy."[1] Note the horse is leaping and skipping *for joy*, and the flight of the swallow *is cheerful*. The heart of God's War Horse is full of joy which is expressed by its dancing.

When Nahum prophesied of the fall of the city of Nineveh, he said they'd hear *"the crack of whips, the noise of the clatter of wheels,* **of the prancing (i.e., dahar) horses***, and dancing, jumping war chariots"* (Nah. 3:2 NIV/KJV/ERRB). There's a lot here, but we'll only focus on the prancing of the horses. We can envision these horses like Tennessee Walkers holding their heads up high, strutting their stuff as they gallop past.

The Hebrew word for prancing is *dahar* (pronounced dawhar) which means "to quickly go in a circle, to rush, gallop, dash, and endure."[2] The primary meaning of this word is *"to go in a circle"* and refers to the custom of breaking or exercising horses by having them run in a circle in the corral. This word also reminds us of our round dance.

A few synonyms for prance are jump, bound, leap, spring, gambol, and skip. A horse's prancing (i.e., *dahar*) is how they dance in the natural realm. But the word picture definition of *dahar* reveals what's going on in the spiritual realm when War Horses dance!

The Hebrew letters in *dahar* are *dalet, hey,* and *resh* and can literally mean "the pathway or door into the revelation of the Most High."[3] When God's War Horses prance, they're literally dancing on the pathway, prancing through the door into God's revelation. The more they dance, the more revelation they receive. So prance, War Horses. Dance and receive God's revelation!

God's War Horses not only prance and do the round dance, but they also love to leap. God asks Job, *"Do you give the horse his might? Is it by your hand that his neck is clothed with power and thunder?* ***Did you give him the ability to jump, leap (i.e., ra' ash) like a grasshopper****, and strike terror with his proud snorting?"* (Job 39:19-20 NASB/BBE/KJV/NIV). The Hebrew word for jump and leap is *ra' ash* (pronounced raw-ash) and means "to shake and tremble (with fear)" or "to leap and spring (like a horse)."[4] It also refers to the shaking caused by an earthquake and how the land shakes when God appears (See Judg. 5:4; Psa. 18:7; Jer. 10:10).

The King James Version mistakenly translates *ra' ash* as *"afraid like a grasshopper,"* but the context is the horse's power and terrifying snorting. Most versions correct this mistake and translate it ***"leap or jump** as a grasshopper."* The War Horse may be trembling, but it's not with fear; it's shaking with excitement at the coming battle! Here's how you know God's transformed you into His War Horse. *If you get excited thinking about the coming conflict,* realize this is *not* normal behavior. Most of us want to avoid conflict! If you react this way to combat, you're a bona fide War Horse.

If anyone is *trembling with fear*, it's the enemy who hears the War Horses coming! In the days of Jeremiah, Israel had rebelled against the Lord and was experiencing His judgment. The prophet says, *"From Dan in the north is heard the snorting of the enemies' war horses.* **At the neighing of his war horses, all the land is shaking with fear (i.e., ra' ash);** *for they have come to devour the whole land and all that is in it"* (Jer. 8:16 NASB/NLT/BBE/NKJV). The whole earth is shaking. This is the physical effect War Horses have in the natural realm. Imagine the *supernatural earthquake shaking* God's War Horses cause in the spiritual realm.

> God's dancing War Horses cause God's supernatural earthquakes.

When Ezekiel prophesies of the destruction of Tyre by Babylonian soldiers, he says, "[T]he hooves of his cavalry will cover you and choke the city with dust. **Your walls will tremble (i.e., ra' ash) from the noise as the war horses** *gallop through your broken gates and walls"* (Ezek. 26:10 NLT/NIV). Once again, a battle in the natural realm reveals what occurs in a battle in the spiritual realm. God's galloping dancing War Horses bring His supernatural earthquake to the kingdoms of this world. The walls of the enemy's strongholds shake and break. The enemy hears God's War Horses coming and trembles with fear.

The Lord tells Job the only time His War Horse trembles is when it's trembling with excitement as it's racing towards the battle. God says His War Horse ***"quivers with frenzied excitement, shaking with passion*** *and rage, he races over the ground and rushes forward into battle when the trumpet is blown"* (Job 39:24 MSG/NIV/BBE/NLT). The words translated *"quivers"* or *"shaking"* is a derivative of *ra' ash*. These two words are spelled the same but have different punctuation marks to distinguish them. This derivative refers to the "confusion, uproar, noise, and tumult of chariots, of horses running, and the crashing in an earthquake."[5] Both words portray the noise and great shaking in a battle or earthquake. The word picture definition of these two words is the same and reveals the cause of this shaking and uproar in the Spirit.

Their Hebrew letters are *resh, ayin,* and *sheen*. They can literally mean "to see, know, and experience the destruction of the Most High."[6] This is why God's War Horses tremble (i.e.. *ra' ash*) with excitement. They *know* they're the weapon God uses *to bring His destruction* upon His enemies. Our enemies tremble and shake (i.e., *ra' ash*) with fear because they *see* the War Horses coming and *know* they're about *to experience God's destruction!*

God trains His War Horses *to run towards the battle*. When we hear the sounds of war: gunshots, bombs exploding, people screaming; we naturally want to run the other way.

> Only God can change our heart, so we'll race into the face of death.

Only the Lord can change our heart, so we'll race into the face of danger and death.

Men and women who serve in the military, police force, firefighters, first-responders, etc., know what it's like to experience fear when facing a dangerous situation. However, their training gives them the ability to overcome this normal reaction. By focusing on their assigned responsibilities to accomplish their goal, they can *ignore* the fear as they advance *into* harm's way. It's the same with God's War Horses. Holy Ghost trains us to focus on the specific part we play to fulfill God's mission, whether it's to worship, pray, confess the Word, dance, etc. In the shock of battle, our training *kicks in.* Because our focus is on Jesus and the task He's assigned us, fear loses its effect. We charge *into* the fray as God's *storm-troopers* and hit the ground running like War Horses.

GOD'S WAR HORSES BRING IN JESUS, OUR WARRIOR KING

God's enemies tremble with fear when they hear God's War Horses coming because they know God's War Horses bear Jesus, God's Warrior King! When Jesus goes to war, He rides a War Horse (Rev. 19:11). God created His War Horse to carry His Warrior King onto the battlefield.

We don't have to wait until the end of the world before we see Jesus go to war. He's been fighting on our behalf ever since He ascended to the right hand of the Father. Since that day, Jesus has interceded for us from heaven (Rom. 8:34), and His Spirit has fought for us on earth in the spiritual realm. The perfect vessel to carry the Spirit of Jesus onto the battlefield is the War Horse of God. The goal of everyone trained in God's Holy Ghost boot camp is to become a War Horse, and when our training is complete, wherever God leads us, we'll run toward the battle.

The Lord says the War Horse *"paws the ground fiercely **and rejoices (i.e., suws) in its strength, when it charges into the fray**, when it gallops to meet the armed men and clash of the weapons. **He mocks at fear, afraid of nothing;** nor does he shy away from the sword"* (Job 39:21-22 MSG/NKJV/NRSV/NIV). The Hebrew word for rejoice is *suws* and means "to be bright, to be cheerful, be glad, and to rejoice by leaping and springing."[7] Again, we see War Horses love to dance by leaping and springing about. They dance with joy and laugh at fear for they are *"bright and cheerful"* with God's glory.

In the midst of battle, War Horses are happy because they know it's never about them. It is all about the One they carry.[8] They rejoice in God's victory, for they've been transformed into His War Horse to transport Jesus, the King of Glory, onto the battleground!

God's War Horse *"**laughing at fear** ... rush towards the battle"* (Job 39:22 CEV/ERV).

> *War Horses rejoice in battle because they're transporting the King onto the battlefield.*

The Hebrew word for laugh is *sachaq* and means "to laugh (usually in contempt or derision, to make sport of, to jest, scorn, and to play (a musical instrument, sing, or dance)."[9] This word describes God laughing at His enemies (Psa. 2:4; 37:13; 59:8). War Horses laugh at fear because they hear their heavenly Rider laughing! Both Horse and Rider know victory is assured.

The Lord concludes His description of the War Horse to Job: *"The blasts of the shofar fill him with courage.* **He laughs, 'Aha.'** *He smells the battle from far away. He hears the thunder of the captains and* **the officers shouting the battle cry**" (Job 39:25 JUB/KJV/GNT/NLV/HCSB). Note two things: 1) the blasts of the Shofar fill us with courage. Spiritual power is released through God's War Horn. 2) God's War Horse is always laughing. As God's War Horse, we're full of joy. We can't stop laughing, especially when we smell and hear the sounds of battle.

The Hebrew word for Aha is *heach* (pronounced heh-awk) and means "a cry of joy used in glorying over an enemy's misfortune."[10] Its word picture tells us why the War Horse laughs so much. Its Hebrew letters *hey, alef, and chet* can literally mean "to have the revelation you are protected and surrounded by God's power."[11] No wonder the War Horse is always laughing!

When we truly realize we're surrounded and protected by God's power, we'll be laughing too. God's War Horses dance by leaping, jumping, hopping, skipping, and going in a circle. The whole time we're dancing, we're laughing as we fight. We're shouting "Aha!" as we go into battle because we know we're protected by the power of God.

> *Surrounded by God's power, we laugh all the time.*

GOD'S DANCING WAR HORSES DESTROY BABYLON

One last War Dance for God's War Horses is revealed in the Hebrew word *'alaz* (pronounced aw-laz) and means "to rejoice, triumph, to be joyful, to leap, jump for joy, and dance."¹² This leaping, jumping War Dance is a perfect fit for God's War Horses.

'Alaz is used in seven Psalms.¹³ Here is one example: *"The Lord is my strength and my shield; my heart trusted in Him, and I am helped.* **Now I'm jumping for joy, my heart greatly rejoices [and] leaps for joy (i.e., 'alaz).** *I burst out with songs of thanksgiving. Save Your people and bless Your inheritance.* **Be their Shepherd and carry them forever**" (Psa. 28:7, 9 NKJV/MSG/NIV/NLT). *'Alaz* is translated *"jump for joy, my heart rejoices and leaps for joy."* It means all of them. War Horses rejoice, jump, and leap for joy because God is their Shepherd.

Psalm 28 concludes with a plea for God to be their Shepherd. This is interesting because *'alaz* is connected with the Shepherd. Its Hebrew letters *ayin, lamed,* and *zayin* can literally mean "to see, know, and experience the Rod of the Shepherd as a weapon."¹⁴ This is beautiful. Jesus, our Shepherd, has a weapon. It's a Rod that explodes with authority. Jesus doesn't use His Rod to beat the sheep but to beat His enemies and protect His sheep. This is another reason we jump and leap for joy (i.e. *'alaz*) in this War Dance. But there's more about our Shepherd's Rod!

David knew all about his shepherd's rod. He used it to kill the lion and bear that attacked his sheep (1 Sam. 17:36). The Hebrew word for rod is *shebet* (pronounced shay-bet) and refers to a "rod, staff, club, scepter, and tribe."¹⁵ The word picture definition of *shebet* explains its power. Its Hebrew letters are *sheen, bet,* and *tet.* They can literally mean what "destroys the house of the serpent."¹⁶ The Rod of God is the Word of God that comes out of Jesus' mouth (Isa. 11:4). Speak the Word of God out of your mouth! When you do, the spoken Word becomes the Rod of God and destroys the house of the serpent. As his evil kingdom falls, we jump and leap with joy!

God's spoken Word becomes a Rod that shatters the house of the serpent.

The prophet Habakkuk uses *'alaz* as the Lord rides His War Horses and war chariots. He asks the Lord, *"Were You angry with the rivers, O LORD… Did You rage against the sea when **You rode on Your horses, on your war chariots of salvation?**"* (Hab. 3:8 NIV/BBE/NET). God is coming, and no matter what happens, Habakkuk declares, *"Yet **I will rejoice, jump for joy (i.e., 'alaz) in the LORD, I will rejoice, twirl, and turn cartwheels of joy (i.e., giyl)** in the God of my salvation"* (Hab. 3:18 NKJV/MSG/ERRB). The two different words for rejoice are *'alaz* and *giyl,* and both mean to dance. *'Alaz* is the War Dance for God's War Horse to rejoice in the power of His Shepherd's Rod, while *giyl* is our War Dance of going in circles and leaping for joy. Jesus is coming back, and He's riding a War Horse. We celebrate His return by dancing. We rejoice by going in a circle, leaping, jumping, and doing cartwheels.

As we wait for Jesus to return, we won't stop dancing. We are God's War Horse. Not only will we run with the foot soldiers and not be weary, we will also race and compete against horses (Jer. 12:5). We will dance and prance all the way to the finish line!

ENDNOTES

1. The Hebrew word *cuwc* is Strong's H5483 at: http://www.blbclassic.org/lang/lexicon/lexicon.cfm?strongs=H5483&t=KJV.
2. The Hebrew word *dahar* is Strong's H1725 at: http://www.blbclassic.org/lang/lexicon/lexicon.cfm?Strongs=H1725&t=KJV.
3. Seekins, pp. 10-11.
4. The Hebrew word *ra' ash* is Strong's H7493 at: http://www.blbclassic.org/lang/lexicon/lexicon.cfm?strongs=H7493&t=KJV.
5. The Hebrew word *ra' ash* is Strong's H7494 at: http://www.blbclassic.org/lang/lexicon/lexicon.cfm?Strongs=H7494&t=KJV.
6. Seekins, pp. 10-11.
7. The Hebrew word *suws* is Strong's H7797 at: http://www.blbclassic.org/lang/lexicon/lexicon.cfm?Strongs=H7797&t=KJV.
8. I love the story about the donkey that carried Jesus into Jerusalem. He went home later that day and bragged to all his donkey friends on how the people went crazy over him as he strolled into the city. But the next day as he went into town, no one even noticed him. Depressed, he returned to his friends and complained about being rejected. An old wise donkey replied, "The people were not cheering for you yesterday; they were cheering for Jesus Whom you were carrying." Moral of the story: without Jesus, we're all just a jackass!
9. The Hebrew word *sachaq* is Strong's H7832 at: http://www.blbclassic.org/lang/lexicon/lexicon.cfm?Strongs=H7832&t=KJV.
10. The Hebrew word *heach* is Strong's H1889 at: http://www.blbclassic.org/lang/lexicon/lexicon.cfm?Strongs=H1889&t=KJV.
11. Seekins, pp. 10-11.
12. The Hebrew word *'alaz* is Strong's H5937 at: www.blbclassic.org/lang/lexicon/lexicon.cfm?Strongs=H5937&t=KJV.
13. The seven Psalms where *'alaz* is used are: 28:7; 60:6; 68:4; 94:3; 96:12; 108:7; & 149:5.
14. Seekins, pp. 10-11.
15. The Hebrew word *shebet* is Strong's H7626 at: www.blbclassic.org/lang/lexicon/lexicon.cfm?strongs=H7626.
16. Seekins, pp. 10-11.

CHAPTER NINE

The Bride's Sword-Dance of the Open Portal

*The Shulamite Bride asks, "Why would
You want to see me dance?"
The Bridegroom-King answers, "Because you dance
so gracefully, as though you danced with angels, **a
sword-dance of joyous victory** as you whirl in **the
round dance of two swords** between two armies."*

SoS. 6:13 tPt/BBE/Voice/CEB/ERRB/NLT

The Most Excellent Love Song

The love song *Dance With Me* by Paul Wilbur is powerful. It begins, *"Dance with me O Lover of my soul,"* and immediately and intimately, it draws you into Jesus' presence. It's perfect for slow dancing with your spouse as you worship the Lord together. The next dance we'll study is a dance of love and warfare—we're going to battle on behalf of our divine Lover.

A beautiful song about the love between a bride and bridegroom is *"The Song of Songs ... Solomon's most excellent Love Song"* (SoS. 1:1 NRSV/NET). It can apply to three different relationships.

- It can be about the love Solomon and his Shulamite bride have for each other.
- It can apply to the love between God and His bride Israel.
- And it can apply to the love Jesus and His Bride, the Church, have for each other.

We'll study this song in reference to Solomon and the Shulamite and see how their love reflects the love of Jesus and His Bride.

The marriage of King Solomon and the Shulamite is built on a covenant of peace. The Hebrew word for Solomon is *Shelomah* which means "peace and peaceful."[1] The letter-by-letter definition of Solomon's name reveals why he is full of peace. Its Hebrew letters *sheen, lamed, mem,* and *hey* can literally mean one who has "the revelation the Shepherd destroys chaos."[2] When David named him Solomon, he was prophesying his son would be full of peace and bring peace.

David taught Solomon that the Lord was his Shepherd (Psa. 23:1) and that this Shepherd destroys chaos. This is powerful. *Chaos is the fruit of demonic activity.* When we fully grasp the revelation that Jesus is our Great Shepherd (Heb. 13:20) and has destroyed all demonic chaos, we'll be like Solomon. Because Jesus is our Great Shepherd, our life, marriage, and home are peaceful. We'll give out His peace to others until our whole nation is living in peace.

Solomon calls his bride *"the Shulamite"* (SoS. 6:13 KJV), which is a pet name.[3] It is the feminine form of his name. In Hebrew, it is *Shuwlammiyth* (pronounced shoo-lam-meth) and means "the peaceful one, the perfect one without spot or blemish."[4] The word picture definition of her name explains why she is peaceful like her bridegroom. The Hebrew letters *sheen, vav, lamed, mem, yod,* and *tav* can literally mean in "covenant with the Shepherd whose nail destroys chaos."[5] Walking in covenant with Solomon, she is one with him. She walks in his peace and becomes the peaceful one. But there is more here besides Solomon and his Shulamite bride.

The Shulamite is perfect without spot or blemish and is a reflection of the Bride of Christ (Eph. 5:27). Like the Shulamite, as we walk in covenant with Jesus, our Great Shepherd, we walk not only in His peace but also in His power and the *power of His nail*. The nail refers to the nails of the Cross, which released the blood of the Lamb of God. The blood of the Shepherd, the Lamb of God, destroys all chaos (Rev. 12:11). Walking in covenant with Jesus, we are one with Him. Walking in the power of His blood released by His nail fills us with His peace.

When We're in Love, We Love to Dance

We're ecstatic when we're in love, and we've got to get those emotions out! One of the best ways to release our joy is by dancing. Solomon is in love; the Shulamite is in love, and all their friends are watching them rejoice, seeing their passion. They exclaim, *"How happy we are for him.* **We will rejoice, twirl**

(i.e., giyl) in you and be glad. *We'll celebrate, we'll sing, we'll make great music. We will extol your love more than wine"* (SoS. 1:4 NLT/NASB/EXE/MSG). We know this word for rejoice. It's the word *giyl*, the dance of joy: spinning, leaping, and going in a circle. The friends of Solomon and the Shulamite are so happy that they had to dance. Seeing such divine love displayed produces that same joy and desire to dance in us.

The love between Solomon and the Shulamite is so obvious their friends see it, and it's so glorious it causes them to rejoice and dance. It's the same with the love between Jesus and His Bride, the Church. Their love will be so obvious that the world will clearly see it. Their love will be a glorious sight, and everyone who sees it will rejoice and dance. There will be an explosion of divine love, a chain reaction of dancing all over the nations as others join the Bride in her dance of joy. Before Jesus returns, the entire world will be dancing, and it starts because Jesus is dancing!

Jesus Loves to Dance

Jesus, our Divine Lover, loves to dance! The Shulamite cries out, *"Listen! I hear my Lover's voice. Look!* **Here He comes leaping (i.e., dalag) over the mountains, skipping (i.e., qaphats) over the hills** *that separate us, to come to me. He is graceful as a gazelle – swift as a wild stag"* (SoS. 2:8-9 NET/tPt/NKJV). In Hebrew, the word for leaping is *dalag*, which we have already studied. It is the same word David used to declare that by God's power, he can leap over a wall. David could do this because God had given him the feet of a wild stag (Psa. 18:29, 33). Jesus and David are wild stags. Both love to leap and skip over every obstacle in their way. Jesus desires to make us a wild stag (Hab. 3:19), so we can join Him in dancing over every blockade.

THE BRIDE'S SWORD-DANCE OF THE OPEN PORTAL | 109

The Hebrew word for skip is *qaphats* and has many meanings. In this verse, it means "to leap, skip, and spring."[6] Jesus likes to dance. David compares Jesus, our Bridegroom, to the sun. David proclaims, *"[T]he heavens declare the glory of God ... the morning sun is like a newly married husband leaping from his honeymoon bed, radiant* **as a bridegroom** *coming out of his chamber,* **like a champion, a warrior rejoicing (i.e., suws) happy and eager to run his course.** *It emerges from one end of heaven, and goes from one end of the sky to the other; nothing is hidden from its heat"* (Psa. 19:1, 5-6 KJV/MSG/tPt / TLB/CEB/NLV/NLT/NET). The word for rejoicing is *suws*, which we have studied earlier. It means "to rejoice and be glad by leaping and springing." In this song, David gives us a beautiful image of Jesus our Bridegroom as the Sun of Righteousness. Like a Champion, a Warrior, He is excited to run around the earth every day.

Jesus sits at the Father's right hand (Rom. 8:34), but His Spirit revolves around the earth like the natural sun. As the Sun of Righteousness, He loves to dance around the planet. The Spirit of Jesus is a Warrior who eagerly encircles our world, leaping and skipping all day and all night! No wonder sunrises and sunsets are so magnificent. They display His glorious ride.

> *Like the Sun, Jesus loves to dance around the earth all day and night.*

Bridegrooms love to dance for their bride. Isaiah says when the Lord restores Zion, *"her righteousness shines out like the dawn and her salvation like a blazing torch"* (Isa. 62:1 NIV). On that day, God will take Israel for His bride, *"For as a young man takes a virgin for his wife, so will* **your Maker be married to you**; *and as a husband rejoices over his bride,* **so will the Lord your God rejoice (i.e., suws) over you**" (Isa. 62:5 BBE/NASB).

On that happy day, the Lord will rejoice; He will leap and spring about His people like a brand-new husband.

Jesus loves to dance with His Bride. He also loves to watch her dance. There's one dance she dances that our Bridegroom-King really enjoys. That dance is a War Dance.

Jesus Loves Watching Us Dance a War Dance

In the Song of Songs, the Shulamite asks her Lover, *"'Why would You want to see me dance?'* The Bridegroom-King answers, *'Because you dance so gracefully, as though you danced with angels,* **a sword-dance of joyous victory** *as you whirl in* **the round dance of two swords** *between two armies. Everyone loves to watch the Shulamite dance her victory dances of love and peace'"* SoS. 6:13 tPt/BBE/Voice/CEB/NLT/CEB/ERRB/MSG). Jesus loves to watch His Bride dance because we dance so gracefully. The dance He enjoys watching the most is our "sword–dance of joyous victory," Think about that, Jesus really loves our War Dance of two swords!

Jesus loves to watch us dance. He really enjoys our War Dance!

One Bible version translates the end of this verse as *"the company of two armies"* (KJV). It should be translated dance and not company because the Hebrew word used here for company is *mechowlah*, which we've studied earlier. It means "to dance." It is the word used for Miriam's dance as God destroyed Pharaoh and his army at the Red Sea (Ex. 15:20). This is the dance of the daughter of Jephthah as she celebrated her father's defeat of the Ammonites (Jud. 11:34), and the dance of the women of Israel as they rejoiced in David killing his ten thousand (1 Sam. 18:6). It is the same word used for the dance of the Shulamite (SoS. 6:13). Like these women warriors listed, she dances a War Dance to celebrate the victories of her Bridegroom–King.

This word *mechowlah* for dancing is the feminine form of *machowl*, which we have also studied. *Machowl* is one of our "round dances" that expresses the joy in our salvation (Jer. 31:4, 13). It's the dance we dance with a two-edged sword in our hand to bind demonic enemies with *"the chains"* of God (Psa. 149:3-9). The Shulamite dances in the double portion anointing. She holds *a two-edged sword in both hands* as she whirls around in her sword-dance of victory.

Some Bibles translate the last word of this verse as *"the Mahanaim"* (NET/NIV), which is the English transliteration of the Hebrew word *machaneh* (pronounced mak-an-eh). This word means a "camp or army" that can include "soldiers, dancers, cattle, locust, stars, and the hosts of heaven."[7] It's the word commonly used for army in the Old Testament and includes the army of stars and God's angel army. The dual form of *machaneh* is the word *machanayin*, which means "two camps."[8] The Hebrew letters in *machanayin* are *mem, chet, nun, yod,* and *mem*. They can literally mean "the life surrounded by mighty power produces works of power."[9] This applies to God's army of angels. Surrounded by God's power, they produce His works of power! It also applies to God's Army of human warriors, who produce His powerful works by His power.

The first time these two words: *machaneh* (i.e., army) and *machanayin* (i.e., two armies), are used in the Old Testament, they are found together. It's when Jacob, after twenty years, was able to return home and see his brother Esau. *"As Jacob went on his way,* **the angels of God** *met him. When Jacob saw them,* *he exclaimed, 'This is the camp, the army (i.e., machaneh) of God!' so he named the place Mahanaim (i.e., machanayin) which means 'two armies or two camps'"* (Gen. 32:1-2 NRSV/ NET/BBE/KJV/Voice/Amp). Jacob sees *"the angels of God"* and knows this is God's Army of angelic warriors because he has seen them before – in a dream.

This phrase *"the angels of God"* is used only one other time in the Old Testament[10] when Jacob *"had a dream in which he saw a ladder, a stairway erected on earth with its top reaching to the heavens.* **The angels of God** *were ascending and descending on it"* (Gen. 28:12 NIV/NET/NASB). Jacob woke up and exclaimed, *"'GOD is in this place, and I did not know it.' Terrified and overwhelmed he said, 'How awesome is this place! I have stumbled into the very house of God!* **This place is a portal,** *the very gate of heaven!"* (Gen. 28:16-17 MSG/KJV/tPt). Jacob realized he was in a very special place—an open portal into the very presence of God!

This ladder, our *"stairway to heaven,"* is Jesus. When Jesus talked to Nathanael and Phillip, He told them they would *"see greater things ... you will see heaven open and* **the angels of God ascending and descending on the Son of Man"** (John 1:50-51 NIV). Jesus quoted this revelation in Jacob's dream because it applied to Him. Jesus was declaring He is the ladder in Jacob's dream. Jesus is the stairway, the gate, the open portal that brings us into the presence of God the Father.

The dance of the Shulamite is called the Mahanaim for a reason. This place Jacob calls Mahanaim (Gen. 32:2) is full of revelation:

1. Jesus is our only way. He is the only ladder that brings us into the presence of God the Father.

2. It is full of military imagery because it focuses on two military camps. One camp is God's Army of angelic warriors, and the other camp is Jacob's warriors.[11]

3. This is the place where God's two Armies are joined together to fight as one.

These *"two camps"* are the Lord's two Armies—one in the natural and the other in the supernatural. One Army is filled with the host of God's angels from heaven, and the other Army is filled with men and women warriors from earth. United, they fight as one to extend God's Kingdom, His rule on earth. The Bride's War Dance opens the portal and activates this union of God's two Armies.

> The Bride's War Dance opens the portal and activates the union of God's two Armies.

The Bride's War Dance of the Open Portal

With the foundation laid, we can now look at *"the dance of Mahanaim,"* our sword-dance of victory. With a sword in each hand, the Warrior Bride of Christ whirls and dances between the two camps to bless and honor her Bridegroom-King. She leads God's people in worship, and the angels join us to glorify the Lord Almighty.

Like Miriam, Jephthah's daughter, and the women of Israel, the Shulamite celebrates in the many victories of her Bridegroom-King over His enemies. Surrounded by the two camps of God's warriors, she ascends her *stairway* into the presence of the Father. Jesus, our Warrior-King, watches with joy as we rejoice in His love and triumph.

I need to share a personal story. A friend of mine was devastated when she learned one of her sons had been sexually molested by their babysitter. Her grief and anger were unbearable. One day at church, she was struggling with her emotions when the Lord told her to dance. She told Him, "I do NOT feel like dancing. I do NOT want to dance!" After more gentle prodding, she got out in the aisle and began to dance. She gave her hurt and bitterness to the Lord as she whirled around and around. The more she twirled, the more the hurts flew off of her.

After the service, a lady came up to her weeping and said, "As I watched you dance, I saw angels all around you. They were going up and down over you. Wherever you went, they went." My friend danced a dance of two swords that cut the wounds and anger away from her heart. Her dance of love was also a dance of war as the wounds of the enemy were healed. This hurting mother danced the dance of the Mahanaim. She opened the portal of heaven to allow God's angels to come and dance with her as she entered into the healing presence of God.

May we hear our Bridegroom-King encourage us to dance with all our hearts. *"The Lover to His Beloved: 'Turn, turn, O Perfect One! Turn; turn that I may gaze on you!* **Dance, dance, dear Shulamite, Angel-Princess! Dance,** *and we'll feast our eyes on your grace'"* (SoS. 6:13a NET/NIV/MSG). The Hebrew word for turn or dance is *shuwb* and means "to turn, to turn about, and to return."[12] This word is used for Arabic tribal dances. The Bridegroom encourages His Beloved, "Spin, spin around for Me!" This is why some Bible versions translate *shuwb* as dance. *"Dance! Dance! Beautiful woman from Shulam* *let us see you dance!"* (CEV/GNT/MSG). Jesus loves watching us dance, especially a War Dance.

The Song of Songs ends with the bride and Bridegroom rejoicing in their love. The bride cries out, *"Arise, my darling! Come quickly, my Beloved. Come and run like the graceful gazelle with me.* ***Come and leap like a wild stag, be a dancing young deer with me. We will dance in the high place of the sky,*** *Yes, on the mountains of fragrant spice. Forever we shall be united as one!"* (SoS. 8:14 tPt/GW/MSG). We will dance with our Divine Warrior in the high place of the sky, united forever as one. What a gorgeous picture of love and glory!

If you don't know how to dance, now is the time to learn. If your church does not dance, now is a good time to start! If the leadership in your church does not allow Holy Ghost dancing, then it may be time to move on. The day for the Church to dance is here, and "The Age of the War Dancing Church" has begun.

Bride of Christ, dance with your Lover in the sky. Usher in "The Age of the War Dancing Church!"

ENDNOTES

1. The Hebrew name *Shelomah* is Strong's H8010 at: http://www.blbclassic.org/lang/lexicon/lexicon.cfm?Strongs=H8010&t=KJV.
2. Seekins, pp. 10-11.
3. Footnote to SoS 6:13 in the TNIV Study Bible.
4. The Hebrew name *Shuwlammiyth* is Strong's H7759 at: http://www.blbclassic.org/lang/lexicon/lexicon.cfm?Strongs=H7759&t=KJV.
5. Seekins, pp. 10-11.
6. The Hebrew word *qaphats* is Strong's H7092 at: http://www.blbclassic.org/lang/lexicon/lexicon.cfm?Strongs=H7092&t=KJV.
7. The Hebrew word *machaneh* is Strong's H4264 at: http://www.blbclassic.org/lang/lexicon/lexicon.cfm?Strongs=H4264&t=KJV.
8. The Hebrew word *machanayin* is Strong's H4266 at: http://www.blbclassic.org/lang/lexicon/lexicon.cfm?Strongs=H4266&t=KJV .
9. Seekins, pp. 10-11 and Benner, p. 127.
10. Footnote to Gen. 32:2 in the NET Bible.
11. Footnote to SoS 6:13 in the NET Bible.
12. The Hebrew word *shuwb* is Strong's H7725 at: http://www.blbclassic.org/lang/lexicon/lexicon.cfm?Strongs=H7725&t=KJV.

CHAPTER TEN

WAR DANCES EXALTING THE MESSIAH AND HIS SALVATION

Jesus rejoiced, jumped for joy in the Holy Spirit, and said, "I thank You, Father, Lord of heaven and earth, for hiding these things from wise and intelligent people and revealing them to little children."
Luke 10:21 ERRB/NASB/NOG

A BABY DANCES WITH JOY

So far, we have mostly studied the dances found in the Old Testament. As we look at New Testament dances, we'll discover that babies like to dance. After the angel Gabriel told Mary she would be a mother, she visited her cousin Elizabeth who was six months pregnant.

"When Elizabeth heard Mary's greeting, **the baby leaped, jumped, and kicked (i.e., skirtao) in her womb**. And Elizabeth was filled with the Holy Spirit" (Luke 1:41 NET/tPt). The Greek word for leap and jump is *skirtao* (pronounced sker-tah-o) and means "to skip, jump, and leap for joy."[1] The baby was John the Baptist, who was *"filled with the Holy Spirit while yet in his mother's womb"* (Luke 1:15 NASB). Mary was pregnant with Jesus (Luke 1:45 CW), and because John was filled with the Holy Spirit, he could detect and respond to the presence of Jesus in Mary's womb.

Filled with the Holy Ghost and joy, Elizabeth, with a loud voice, *"prophesied with power: 'Mary! Blessed are you among women, and blessed is the fruit of your womb. For the instant you came in the door and greeted me,* **my baby leaped [and] jumped for joy ... skipped like a lamb ... danced (i.e., skirtao) inside me with ecstatic joy!**'" (Luke 1:42, 44 tPt/NKJV/NLT/MSG). The word for leaped, jumped, skipped, and danced is *skirtao*. John, *the baby*, was being prepared very early to become John *the Baptist* and reveal the Messiah to the world.

When my wife Sharon was pregnant with our second son Seth, she went to a prayer meeting. Some people prayed for her, and she got slain in the Spirit. As she was lying on the floor, little Seth started dancing like crazy in her womb. He's still dancing like crazy today. If unborn children *inside the womb* can detect the presence of God's Spirit and respond by dancing, then people *outside the womb*, when in the presence of God's Spirit, can do the same.

Skirtao is found one more time in the New Testament when Jesus delivers the Sermon on the Mount. Jesus told His followers, *"Blessed are you when people hate you, when they exclude you and insult you and reject you and cast out your name as evil because of your love for Me, the Son of Man!* **When that** *happens, rejoice! Yes, leap, jump (i.e., skirtao) for joy! For your reward in heaven will be great"* (Luke 6:22-23 NKJV/NET/tPt/BBE). I love two translations here: *"[Y]ou will celebrate and **dance with overflowing joy**. Skip like a lamb, if you like! – **for even though they don't like it, I do … and all heaven applauds"** (tPt/MSG). When we're persecuted because we love Jesus, He tells us to celebrate, dance, and skip like lambs.

It doesn't matter if people around us don't like our dancing. Jesus likes it. And when we dance, all heaven applauds. John started dancing early in life! If *little baby John* can dance in the womb, then *really big people* can dance in the world.

If baby John can dance in the womb, then big people can dance in the world.

MARY DANCES TO HER SONG OF THE SAVIOR

Elizabeth prophesied over Mary and informed her that God's Word spoken by Gabriel had been fulfilled. Elizabeth proclaimed, *"Bless you, you have believed the angel and it happened! **You're pregnant!** And all the other things he told you will happen too!"* (Luke 1:45 CW). Surprised and inspired by this glorious news, Mary sang a prophetic song. *"And Mary sang this song: 'My soul magnifies the Lord, **and my spirit rejoices, jumps for joy (i.e., agalliao) in God my Savior'"*** (Luke 1:46-47 tPt/ NKJV/NRSV/ERRB). Like Hannah many years ago (1 Sam. 2:1-10), Mary exalted in the Lord's miracle-working power to bring forth new life supernaturally.

The Greek word for rejoices is *agalliao* (pronounced ag-al-lee-ah-o) and means "to exult, to rejoice and be exceeding glad by jumping for joy."[2] Spiros Zodhiates says *agalliao* means "to exult, to leap for joy, to show one's joy by leaping and skipping denoting excessive or ecstatic joy and delight ... often spoken of rejoicing with song and dance."[3] This is why one translation reads, *"my soul doth magnify the Lord and* **my spirit jumpeth for joy (i.e., agalliao)** *in God my Savior"* (Luke 1:46-47 ERRB). Another says, *"And Mary said, 'I'm bursting with God-news;* **I'm dancing the song of my Savior God'"** (Luke 1:46-47 MSG). I love these translations because they show Mary was dancing and jumping for joy as she sang. *Agalliao* means to rejoice by dancing.

Much of Mary's song, like this last verse, comes from the Psalms, *"my soul shall* **be joyful, twirl (i.e., giyl)** *in the LORD, and* **it shall rejoice (i.e., suws)** *in His salvation"* (Psa. 35:9 NKJV/ERRB). We recognize these Hebrew words for joyful and rejoice. They're our War Dances: *Giyl* means to spin, go in a circle, and leap; and *Suws* means to leap and spring. *Agalliao* is the Greek word in the New Testament that reflects what these two Hebrew words in the Old Testament mean.[4] The word *agalliao* is equivalent to *giyl*. Both mean to rejoice by dancing. *Agalliao* is a War Dance of victory. That means in our New Covenant with Jesus; we have War Dances too.

Jesus Dances in the Spirit

When the disciples come back from the missionary trip where they preached the Kingdom, they *"returned with joy and said, 'Lord, even the demons submit to us in Your name'"* (Luke 10:17 NIV). Jesus told them He saw satan fall like lightning from heaven but instructed them not to rejoice in this authority but to rejoice that their names are recorded in heaven (Luke

10:18-20). Salvation is the main blessing; casting out demons in Jesus' name is a side benefit.

The disciples were rejoicing; now, it was Jesus' turn to rejoice. *"At that very moment,* ***Jesus rejoiced (i.e., agalliao) overflowing with the Holy Spirit's anointing of joy****, and said, 'I praise You, Father, Lord of heaven and earth, that You have hidden these things from the wise and intelligent and have revealed them to infants'"* (Luke 10:21 NABRE/tPt/NASB). ***"Jesus jumped for joy in the Holy Spirit"*** (ERRB). Can you imagine Jesus' joy! Can you see Him jumping up and down with joy? His followers were getting it. They were finally walking in His authority over the enemy!

We're told to build ourselves up *"by praying in the Holy Spirit"* (Jude 1:20 NASB). Here Jesus was *jumping in the Holy Spirit!* Jesus is happy when we take the authority He's given us to rule over our adversaries *"I have given you authority to tread on serpents and scorpions and* ***over all the power of the enemy*** *and nothing will hurt you"* (Luke 10:19 NASB). When we do this, it makes Jesus so happy; He has to dance! If we want to make Jesus jump up and down with joy, start moving in the authority He has given us, and we'll be dancing too!

> Jesus is happy when we take the authority He has given us to rule over our adversaries.

It's a joy to read different Bible versions. When the disciples return and tell Jesus of their authority over demons in His name, it's ironic how the Message Bible describes their triumph. They rejoiced and exclaimed, *"Master, even* ***the demons danced to Your tune!"*** (Luke 10:17). You have to love it. The demons were dancing to Jesus' tune, but it definitely wasn't a happy dance!

DANCING IN OUR NEW COVENANT SALVATION

Here is a list of a few other verses that use *agalliao* and when we're to dance:

1. **People danced for joy at the preaching of John the Baptist.** Jesus said, *"John was a torch that was burning and shining, and **you were willing to rejoice, jump for joy, and dance (i.e., agalliao)** for an hour or so in his bright light"* (John 5:35 MSG/NET/ERRB).

2. **Abraham jumped for joy to see Jesus' day.** Jesus told the religious leaders, *"[Y]our father **Abraham rejoiced, jumped for joy (i.e., agalliao) at the thought of seeing My day**, with jubilant faith [he] looked down the corridors of history and saw My day coming. He saw it and cheered"* (John 8:56 NIV/ERRB/MSG).

3. **At the preaching of Paul and Silas, the Roman jailer and his whole family get saved, got baptized, and jumped for joy.** *"The jailer brought them into his house and set food before them. **He and his entire household rejoiced, leaped much, and jumped for joy (i.e., agalliao)**"* (Acts 16:34 NET/NLT/Amp/ERRB).

4. **Peter encourages us to rejoice and jump for joy during tests and trials.** The day is coming when God's salvation will be revealed. Peter says on that last day we'll *"**greatly rejoice, jump for joy (i.e., agalliao) for all eternity**, even though now, if for a little while you have to suffer various trials. You have never seen Jesus, and you don't see Him now. But still you love Him and have*

*faith in Him and **you greatly rejoice, jump for joy (i.e., agalliao)** with a glorious joy that is beyond words"* (1 Pet. 1:6, 8 MSG/ERRB/MEV/CEV/CJB/tPt with footnote).

5. **There will be dancing at the marriage feast of the Bride and her King.** *"Let us be glad and rejoice, jump for joy (i.e., agalliao) and give Him glory, for the marriage of the Lamb has come, and His wife has made herself ready"* (Rev. 19:7 NKJV/ERRB). Glory!

With our study of *skirtao* and *agalliao*, we see dancing did not stop in the Old Testament. We also dance as we rejoice in our New Covenant. We'll dance at the marriage supper of the Lamb, and we'll keep on dancing throughout eternity.[5] It's time to get in some practice!

Anointed with the Oil of Dancing

The Holy Ghost calls us to dance like Jesus, as we'll discover in the derivative of *agalliao*. The word *agalliasis* (pronounced ag-al-lee-as-is) means "extreme joy, exultation, and gladness."[6] This word often refers to "rejoicing with song, dancing, [and] oil of gladness with which guests were anointed at feasts [and] used as an emblem of the highest honors."[7] As we study *agalliasis* in the New Testament, we'll see it's connected to the word *chagag* in the Old Testament. Recall *chagag* means to dance, to move in a circle, to reel, and to celebrate a feast or festival. Both refer to the Jewish feasts. Being anointed with the oil of gladness at a feast will cause us to celebrate by dancing. This anointing oil and dancing go together.

Here are the five verses where *agalliasis* is used in the New Testament:

- The angel of the Lord told Zechariah that his wife Elizabeth would bear a son. His name will be John, *"and you will have joy **and gladness (i.e., agalliasis)** and many will rejoice at his birth"* (Luke 1:14 NKJV). Two versions translate *agalliasis* this way: John *"**shall be thy cheer and thy jumping for joy**"* (ERRB) and *"**you're going to leap like a gazelle for joy**, and not only you – many will delight in his birth"* (MSG). Zechariah is going to have a baby boy! He rejoices by jumping for joy and leaping like a gazelle. That will get the neighbors talking.

- When Mary visited Elizabeth, she said, *"As soon as I heard the sound of your greeting, 'Shalom' the baby **danced in my womb and jumped for joy (i.e., agalliasis)**"* (Luke 1:44 CEV/CJB/OJB/ERRB). First, it was his father, Zechariah; now, little baby John was jumping. Everyone in this first chapter of Luke was jumping and dancing for joy.

- After the Holy Spirit was poured out on the day of Pentecost, *"the believers had a single purpose. Every day they devoted themselves to meeting together in the temple area and breaking bread from house to house **with great joy, with gladness in jumping for joy (i.e., agalliasis) and thankfulness**"* (Acts 2:46 NOG/NABRE/TLB/ERRB). That's a wild image. Let's see if we can be like these people, eating and jumping at the same time!

- Jude concluded his letter to believers with this blessing: *"Now to Him Who is able to keep you from stumbling, or slipping, or falling and make you stand without blemish before the presence of His glory **jumping with exceeding great joy (i.e., agalliasis)**"* (Jude 1:24 KJV/Amp/HCSB/ERRB). As we walk with Jesus, we don't stumble and fall in defeat; by His power, Jesus makes us stand and jump with joy in His victory.

ANOINTED WITH THE OIL OF JUMPING, JESUS DANCES A WAR DANCE

In Hebrews, there is one more verse that uses *agalliasis*. The writer is revealing Jesus' glory and says, *"You have loved righteousness and hated wickedness; therefore God, Your **God has anointed You with the oil of gladness, the oil of jumping for joy (i.e., agalliasis)** more than Your companions"* (Heb. 1:9 NKJV/NET/NIV/ERRB). God has anointed Jesus with the oil of gladness. This specific anointing makes Him jump for joy!

The writer of Hebrew is quoting from the Psalms, *"You love justice and hate evil. For this reason God, your God has anointed you with the oil of joy, rejoicing, gladness (i.e., sasown) more than on anyone else"* (Psa. 45:7 NET/NLT/ERRB/KJV). The Hebrew word for rejoicing, gladness, and joy is *sasown* (pronounced saw-sone) and means "gladness, cheerfulness, mirth, rejoicing, and joy."[8] It is derived from the root word *suws*, which we learned means to be bright, cheerful, to rejoice, be glad, to leap, and to spring. The images *sasown* and *suws* portray are that when we're cheerful, we shine. We rejoice by leaping and springing about like gazelles, horses, and calves. Now, that's a dance, and it's a happy one!

The context of Psalm 45 reveals this dance is a War Dance celebrating a victory. The Warrior dances because He's just won a battle. *"Now strap Your lightning-sword of judgment on Your side, O mighty Warrior. Ride majestically! Ride triumphantly! You are full of beauty* **as You go out to war! Ride out into battle victorious. Win the victory for truth and mercy and justice.** *Do fearsome things with Your powerful arm. Your sharp arrows penetrate the hearts of the king's enemies.* **Nations are defeated. They fall down at Your feet.** *Your throne is the very throne of God. Your kingdom will last forever. You will rule by treating everyone fairly"* (Psa. 45:3-6 tPt/CEV/MSG/Voice/ICB/ISV/GNT/NIrV). Jesus goes to war and protects His people. His enemies fall at His feet, and His Kingdom will last forever. Jesus jumps for joy as He dances His War Dance of victory.

Ride into war following our Warrior-King. His sword and arrows of glory strike down the enemy. The King establishes His Kingdom forever. As we *"love what is right and hate what is wrong"* (Psa. 45:7 NLT), God will pour out His oil of joy on us. God's holy anointing oil of gladness causes us to dance to celebrate His victory.

Lord, anoint us with Your oil of jumping for joy. We'll dance a War Dance like Jesus. If you say, "I can't dance," God replies, "I have an anointing for that." At least we can jump.

If you say, "I can't dance," God replies, "I have an anointing for that."

ENDNOTES

1. The Greek word *skirtao* is Strong's G4640 at: www.blbclassic.org/lang/lexicon/lexicon.cfm?Strongs=G4640&t=KJV.
2. The Greek word *agalliao* is Strong's G21 at: www.blbclassic.org/lang/lexicon/lexicon.cfm?Strongs=G21&t=KJV.
3. Zodhiates, Spiros. *The Complete Word Study Dictionary: New Testament.* AMG Publishers, Chattanooga, TN. 1992. Page 64.
4. Retrieved from Thayer's Lexicon at: www.blbclassic.org/lang/lexicon/lexicon.cfm?Strongs=G21&t=KJV.
5. Footnote to 1 Pet. 1:6 in the Passion Translation of the Bible.
6. The Greek word *agalliasis* is Strong's G20 at: www.blbclassic.org/lang/lexicon/lexicon.cfm?strongs=G20&t=KJV.
7. Zodhiates, page 63.
8. The Hebrew word *sasown* is Strong's H8342 at: www.blbclassic.org/lang/lexicon/lexicon.cfm?Strongs=H8342&t=KJV.

Chapter Eleven

War Dances Rejoicing in Jesus' Healing Power

Jumping up, he stood and began to walk, and he entered the temple with them walking,
leaping, dancing, and praising God.

Acts 3:8 NRSV/MSG

Jesus' Healing Power Creates Happy, Dancing Feet

Our feet are important in both the natural and spiritual realm. We need our feet—literally—to walk through life. We need them to take possession of our inheritance. God told Moses and the people of Israel, *"Every place on which the sole of your foot treads shall be yours"* (Deut. 11:24 NASB). With our feet, we tread upon the enemy. Jesus promised, *"I have **given***

you authority to trample on snakes and scorpions *and to overcome all the power that the enemy possesses and nothing will harm you"* (Luke 10:19 NIV/Amp). Jesus empowers our feet. He has shod them with *"the gospel of peace"* (Eph. 6:15), so *"the God peace"* can crush satan under our feet (Rom. 16:20). Everywhere our feet, shod with peace, go; the God of peace follows.

One day Peter and John were walking to the temple to pray. Their feet were shod with the Gospel of peace when they saw a man who was crippled from birth. He was sitting at the Beautiful Gate begging for money. Peter did not have any money to give him, but he had the healing power of Jesus. Peter could give him the peace of God.

Peter commanded him in the name of Jesus to rise up and walk. Then Peter grabbed him by the right hand and pulled him up, *"and immediately the man's feet and ankle bones were made strong. He jumped to his feet and began to walk and entered the temple with them –* ***walking, and leaping (i.e., hallomai), and praising God"*** (Acts 3:7-8 NKJV/NIV/NET). The people were astounded as they saw the man *"dancing and praising God"* (MSG). When Jesus heals feet, they become happy, dancing feet.

Healed feet become happy, dancing feet!

I mentioned in an earlier chapter that the people watching were overwhelmed by this miracle. Though not recorded, it is possible that this man *was missing* one or both feet, and Jesus gave him new feet. The Greek word for lame or crippled is *cholos* and means "to be lame, crippled, to limp, maimed, or deprived of a foot."[1] It's the same as the word *anaperos* (pronounced an-ap-ay-ros), which means "to be crippled or maimed" having lost a limb such as a hand, arm, or leg.² *Cholos* refers to missing a foot, while *anaperos* refers to missing a limb such as an arm or leg. No wonder the people were so amazed and the religious leaders so angry with Peter and John. Here's a man who for forty years didn't have one or both feet; now he had new feet and was walking, leaping, dancing, and praising God in the temple!

The Greek word for leaping is *hallomai* (pronounced hal-lom-ahee) and means "to jump, leap, and spring up."³ *Hallomai* is the root word for *agalliao*, which we studied in the last chapter. Both are very similar in meaning. *Hallomai* is used three times in the New Testament: in the Gospel of John and in Acts, where it's used in a story about another man healed of lame feet.

This time Holy Spirit used Paul and Barnabas. They were preaching in Lystra and saw a man listening to them who could not use his feet from birth. He never *"had the power of walking"* (Acts 14:8 BBE). When Paul *"saw the man had faith to be healed, he said with a loud voice, "Stand on your feet!' And* **the man leaped up, jumped up, sprang up (i.e., hallomai) and began walking***" (Acts 14:9-10 NET/NIV/NRSV). Note the power and authority in Paul's voice! He simply said, "Stand on your feet," and the man got up and walked. God really loves to heal crippled feet and change them into dancing feet.

There are many beautiful revelations in this story. The man's feet were impotent (KJV). The Greek word for impotent is *adynatos* (ad-oo-nat-os) and means "to be weak, without power, and disabled."⁴ It also conveys the idea of something being "impossible."⁵ In other words, it was impossible for this man to walk. But what's impossible for us is possible for God.

So here is this man who was in an impossible situation, but look where he was living—the city of Lystra. The Greek word for Lystra is its transliteration *Lystra*. The meaning of this word is uncertain, but all of the possible meanings are awesome. One source says Lystra means "ransoming (i.e., to release a prisoner after making the payment demanded)."[6] Another source says Lystra comes from the verb *luo*, which means "to loose, unbind, or disintegrate."[7] Both are fantastic. This man lived in the city where the *ransom has been paid*, a place where he was *loosed and unbound* from all bondages because they were *disintegrated* in Jesus' blood!

Holy Spirit Is the Source of Our War Dance

The last place *hallomai* is found in the New Testament is in the Gospel of John. Jesus was talking to the Samaritan woman who came to draw water from a well. He said, *"Everyone who drinks some of this water will be thirsty again. But whoever drinks some of the water that I will give him will never be thirsty again, but the water that I will give him **will become in him a fountain of water springing up (i.e., hallomai) to eternal life**"* (John 4:13-14 NET). The Greek word Jesus used for springing up is *hallomai*, and the water gushing out represents the Holy Spirit.

Later at the Feast of Tabernacles, Jesus shouted, *"If anyone is thirsty, let him come to Me and let the one who believes in Me drink. Just as the Scripture says, '**out of his belly shall flow rivers of living water.**' When He said 'living water,' He was speaking of the Spirit, Who would be given to everyone believing in Him. But the Spirit had not been given yet because Jesus was not yet glorified"* (John 7:37-39 NET/NKJV/NLT). When we give our heart to Jesus, He places in us His fountain, a river of supernatural water that comes *rushing, leaping out* of our belly.

It is no accident the Holy Spirit inspires Luke later on to use this same word to describe the jumping and leaping of two men after their feet are healed (Acts 3:7-8 & 14:9-10). By using the same word, the Spirit reveals to us that the living water is the Holy Spirit and is the source of healing our feet. Holy Spirit is also the source of causing our feet to dance. A gushing, leaping (i.e., *hallomai*) river of the Holy Spirit creates our leaping (i.e., *hallomai*), dancing feet.

> *The leaping river of the Spirit in our belly creates the leaping and dancing in our feet.*

These three references reveal that the Lord desires for His children to have healthy, healed feet—happy, dancing, healthy feet. We need healthy feet to tread on the head of the enemy and take back this world for God. Every place we walk, we're taking back one person, one family, one nation at a time for the Lord. So it is good to have strong, healthy, happy feet. Let's dance as we take back the earth for God.

The War Dance Is God's Weapon

Since we're studying leaping in the New Testament, let's also look at two Hebrew words for leap in the Old Testament. One is *pazaz* (pronounced paw- zaz) and means "to bound, leap for joy, spring up, to be strong, nimble, and agile."[8] It's found twice in the Old Testament and is first used by Jacob when he prophesied over his twelve sons. He said Joseph would be an archer whose *"bow will remain steady, **and his arms were made agile, strong, skillful (i.e., pazaz)** by the hands of the Mighty God of Jacob"* (Gen. 49:24 NKJV/NRSV/NET). Here *pazaz* refers to the strength, agility, and skill the hand of God gives to the archers' hands in Joseph's tribe. It also refers to the arrow *leaping* out from the bow.

Pazaz also refers to dancing and is used to describe David's dancing before the Lord. *"As the Ark of the Lord entered the City of David, Michal, the daughter of Saul, looked down from her window and saw King David **jumping, leaping, skipping, hopping (i.e., pazaz)** and dancing, twirling (i.e., karar)before the LORD, and she despised him in her heart"* (2 Sam. 6:16 NLT/BBE/CEB/WYC/ERRB). *Pazaz* refers to David's leaping, and the word for dancing is *karar*. We've studied *karar* earlier. It means to twirl and dance in a circle. Michal may have despised David as he jumped, skipped, whirled, and danced, *but God loved it.*

The word picture definition of *pazaz* gives us a powerful revelation. Its letters *pey, zayin,* and *zayin* can literally mean this dance "is speaking words [and these words] are a weapon that cuts."[9] The art of dancing communicates a message. It tells a story. Talented dancers easily and clearly convey that message to those watching them.

God's revealing that the *pazaz* is a War Dance. The message it gives; the *words it speaks are a weapon that cuts.* It goes perfectly with War Songs. The War Songs are taunt-songs (Isa. 14:4 NCV) that pierce the enemy with the Word of God, and this War Dance adds power to the attack by cutting the enemy with the message of its dance. As the dancers *leap about,* they're releasing the glory of God like arrows *leaping from* a bow.

One last leaping War Dance is revealed in the Hebrew word *zanaq.* It means "to leap like a lion, to dart upon its prey, to spring forward, and to shoot an arrow."[10] It is only used once in the Old Testament when Moses prophesied about the tribe of Dan. *"And of Dan he said: Dan is a lion's cub that **charges** out* *of Bashan. The people of Dan … **pounce** on their enemies. **That leap, jump, and spring forth (i.e., zanaq) from Basham**"* (Deut. 33:22 WEB/NIrV/NOG/NCV). When we leap in our War Dance, we're charging our enemy. Our War Dance is a weapon.

We see this in the word picture definition of *zanaq*. Its Hebrew letters are *zayin, nun,* and *qof.* They can literally mean "the destiny of this life is to be a weapon."[11] God's destiny for our life as His dancing warrior is to be a weapon for Him. When dancing warriors leap as God's lion, they become spiritual weapons in God's hands. Our roar strikes terror in the enemy's camp.

Zanaq, like *pazaz,* also refers to shooting an arrow, like an arrow *leaping* from the bow. In this War Dance, our leaping is a spiritual arrow. Dance a War Dance to the Lord and against His enemies. Let our arrows fly out full of God's power against the evil one.

> God transforms our leaping War Dance into His weapon.

Respond to Holy Ghost Inspired Dancing

We'll return to the New Testament and study one more Greek word for dancing. The word *orcheomai* (pronounced or-khe-om-ahee) is used four times in the Gospels in reference to two different situations, and it means "to dance in a rapid motion, to dance in a row or ring."[12] *Orcheomai* means "to lift up the feet, to leap with regularity of motion."[13] We get our English word orchestra from the Greek word, *orcheomai*. The origin relates to Greek theater, where the "orchestra" was a semi-circular area between the audience and the stage reserved for musicians and dancers. An *orchestre* was an individual dancer or performer. A *choros* was a group of dancers. In modern terms, the orchestra is the group of musicians who play in an orchestra pit (that original semi-circular area called the *orcheomai*).

It's used when Herodias' daughter danced for Herod, *"On Herod's birthday the daughter of Herodias **danced (i.e., orcheomai) before Herod** and greatly pleased him so much that he promised with an oath to give her whatever she asked"* (Matt. 14:6-7 NIV/NLT). She went to her mother and said, *"'[W]hat shall I ask for?' And her mother told her, 'Ask for the head of John the Baptizer'"* (Mark 6:24 NASB/NLT). Herodias had been *"smothering with hate and wanted John killed"* (Mark 6:19 MSG/NLT) because John preached against Herod marrying her because she had been the wife of his brother. Her daughter's dance gave her the chance to get her revenge!

A lot is going on in this story, but all we are concerned about is the realization that dancing has a powerful impact on people. In this situation, the dancing of Herodias' daughter so moved Herod that he made a rash promise. We're not told the specifics of how she danced, but it was definitely not inspired by the Holy Spirit—some other unholy spirit was behind this dance.

The other reference is when Jesus told us about dancing inspired by the Spirit. He asked His disciples, *"How shall I describe this generation? These people are like a group of spoiled children whining to their parents. They complain to their friends, **'We played the pipe for you playing the music of wedding songs, and you weren't happy; you did not take part in the dance (i.e., orcheomai).** We wailed and sang a funeral song, but you weren't sad and did not mourn.' For John didn't drink wine and* he often fasted, and you say, 'He's crazy and demon possessed.' And I, the Son of Man, feast and drink, and you say, 'He's a glutton and a drunkard, and a friend of the worst sort of sinners!' But wisdom is justified, shown to be right by the results from her actions"* (Matt. 11:16-19 NLT/MSG/Amp/NET/BBE/NASB/NIV/NKJV & Luke 7:31-35). Jesus is saying a lot, but we will focus on only two points.

First, Jesus said John came as one playing a dirge, a funeral song, because the people needed to repent and *die to their old nature*. But they refused to mourn and did not repent under the conviction of the Holy Spirit for their sin. Instead, they accused John of being possessed by a demon. Their reaction shows how deceived they were. John was motivated by the Spirit of God, but they did not discern the work of *the Holy Spirit*. They saw it as the work of *an unholy spirit*.

Second, they did not rejoice and dance as Jesus came playing His wedding songs. This was even worse. They did not discern the Holy Spirit moving through Jesus in His love, joy of life, and miracles! They saw Him as a drunk who craved food and loved to spend time with sinners. Jesus was playing a wedding song of love to woo His future Bride to His side. When Jesus is moved by the Spirit and plays a wedding song, we should be inspired by the Spirit to dance. Jesus, our Bridegroom, is playing wedding songs now and saying, "Come dance with Me!" So, let's dance.

> *Jesus is playing His wedding songs and saying, "Come dance with Me!"*

Orcheomai dancing is full of passion and inspiration. In a bad way, the dancing of the daughter of Herodias influenced Herod to the point he had John the Baptist killed. While in a good and powerful way, songs flowing from the

Holy Spirit inspire us to dance and enjoy our Bridegroom. The dance of the flesh and the world brings death. The dance of the Spirit brings life. The dance of life is a War Dance. It conquers the dance of death every time. "Holy Spirit, give us Your discernment to know the difference!"

The War Dance of Life conquers the dance of death every time.

ENDNOTES

1. The Greek word *cholos* is Strong's G5560 at: www.blbclassic.org/lang/lexicon/lexicon.cfm?Strongs=G5560&t=KJV.
2. The Greek word *anaperos* is Strong's G376 at Zodhiates, p. 157 and www.blbclassic.org/lang/lexicon/lexicon.cfm?Strongs=G376&t=KJV.
3. The Greek word hallomai is Strong's G242 at: www.blbclassic.org/lang/lexicon/lexicon.cfm?Strongs=G242&t=KJV.
4. The Greek word adynatos is Strong's G102 at: www.blbclassic.org/lang/lexicon/lexicon.cfm?Strongs=G102&t=KJV.
5. Ibid.
6. The Greek word Lystra is Strong's G3082 at: www.blbclassic.org/lang/lexicon/lexicon.cfm?Strongs=G3082&t=KJV.
7. Retrieved from Abarim Publications at: www.abarim-publications.com/Meaning/Lystra.html.
8. The Hebrew word pazaz is Strong's H6339 at: http://www.blbclassic.org/lang/lexicon/lexicon.cfm?Strongs=H6339&t=KJV.
9. Seekins, pp. 10-11.
10. The Hebrew word zanaq is Strong's H2187 at: http://www.blbclassic.org/lang/lexicon/lexicon.cfm?Strongs=H2187&t=KJV.
11. Seekins, pp. 10-11.
12. The Greek word orcheomai is Strong's G3738 at: www.blbclassic.org/lang/lexicon/lexicon.cfm?Strongs=G3738&t=KJV.
13. Vine's Dictionary at: www.blbclassic.org/lang/lexicon/lexicon.cfm?Strongs=G3738&t=KJV.

CHAPTER TWELVE

The Godhead Loves to Dance with Joy

The LORD your God is in your midst.
He is a mighty, victorious Warrior.
He will exult over you with joy.
With His love He will calm all your fears.
He will twirl over you with shouts of
joy *and singing a happy song.*

Zeph. 3:17 NASB/NLT/ERRB

Jesus Plays Wedding Songs for Us

We studied these verses in the last chapter, but we need to look at another aspect concerning them. When Jesus tells the disciples, *"These people are like a group of spoiled children whining to their parents, they complain to their friends,* **'We played the pipe for you playing wedding songs, and you weren't happy; you did not dance"** (Matt. 11:16-17 NLT/ MSG/Amp/NASB/ NIV). Jesus is warning us about a spirit that opposes Holy Ghost-inspired dancing.

Jesus was angry at the complacency of the people. They wouldn't respond to the work of the Holy Spirit. They wouldn't mourn at John's call to repent and be baptized, nor would they be happy and dance at Jesus's wedding songs. An individual with a religious, legalistic spirit will reject the move of the Holy Spirit.

Religious spirits condemn everything Jesus and His disciples did! They said John had a demon, and Jesus was a drunk. The heart of a person with a religious spirit is deceived and dead. No matter what God's children do, that legalistic demon will twist and pervert their actions and words. This stronghold of religious legalism is established in our land, but take heart; it will fall!

There is a stronghold of dead religion in the city where I live, and God has directed our fellowship to counterattack its effects by dancing. And when I say dance, we *really* dance! We beat our tambourines, shout our War Cries, sound our Shofars, and wave our War Flags as we dance our War Dance. All of us, including the little children, spin, leap, jump, and go in a circle.

Now, the older folks may not jump or leap very high, but they will do a little side-to-side grapevine or an abbreviated *electric slide* or the *hokey-pokey*. They'll put their right foot in, put their right foot out and shake it all about! We'll do whatever the Holy Spirit tells us to drive out the religious demons in this place. We declare, "We've decided to follow

Jesus, and that includes dancing with total abandon with our Bridegroom-King to His wedding songs!"

"Lord, protect us from a cold, condemning heart that was operating inside Micah, David's wife." She judged David's Holy Ghost dancing unto the Lord and despised him. She accused David of being *"just **like any pervert who exposes himself**"* (2 Sam. 6:20 ISV/GW). She thought she was right, and David was wrong, but her infected heart was blind to the truth.

Micah's heart was infested with the fruit of her father, Saul, who loved David's music (1 Sam. 16:23) but despised David's fame (1 Sam. 18:6-9, 25). His hatred and jealousy of David opened the door to a spirit of murder. Living in such a home influenced Micah with a condemning, judgmental spirit. As she watched her husband dance, *"she despised him in her heart"* (2 Sam. 6:16 NASB). The Hebrew word for despised is *bazah*. It means "to despise, hold in contempt, and disdain" someone because you see them as "vile and worthless."[1] Blinded by these spirits, Micah did not see God's anointed *"sweet psalmist of Israel"* (2 Sam. 23:1 KJV). Instead, she was offended because she saw a repulsive and worthless man.

The word picture definition of *bazah* reveals the effects of this spirit of condemnation and judgment. Its Hebrew letters are *bet, zayin,* and *hey* and can literally mean "the family that cuts off revelation."[2] The letter *zayin* represents a weapon like a hatchet or an axe used to cut and hack things. When we despise someone, that judgmental attitude is like an axe or hatchet that cuts off revelation. Micah lived in a family that despised God's anointed one. That spirit had cut off revelation, and she was unable to see the real David.

When a religious, legalistic spirit attacks our heart, the fruit it produces is an attitude of condemnation. We see the older generation complain that the young people's music is irreverent. It's too loud and fast. While the young people complain about the music of the older folks not being fresh. It's too slow and just—old! We need to ask God to protect our hearts and reveal if any legalistic spirit of condemnation has crept in, making our hearts hard or critical. With God's heart, we'll receive with open arms whatever music the Holy Ghost directs us to play and dance whatever He wants us to dance! Everything birthed by God's Spirit, especially dancing, is full of His life and joy.

> Everything birthed by God's Spirit, especially dancing, is full of life and joy.

Jesus Loves to Dance Because the Father Loves to Dance

Jesus told His disciples, *"I tell you the solemn truth, the Son can do nothing by Himself;* **He can only do what he sees the Father doing**, *because whatever the Father does the Son also does"* (John 5:19 NET/NIV). Jesus dances and loves to dance because *He sees the Father dance* and love to dance.

Here are a few verses that reveal the Father loves to dance. Before Joshua led the people of Israel to possess the Promised Land, the Lord renewed the covenant with this new generation (Deut. 29:1). As they were faithful to follow the Lord, Moses gave them this promise from God, *"Then the LORD your* **God will prosper you abundantly in all the work of your hand, God will make you successful in everything you do.** *He will give you many children and numerous livestock, and your fields will produce abundant harvests,* **for the Lord will again rejoice** *(i.e., suws) over you to make you prosperous, just as He rejoiced (i.e., suws) over your ancestors"* (Deut. 30:9 NASB/NLT/NET). Both times the Hebrew word for rejoice is *suws*, which we have studied before and means to rejoice, be glad, cheerful, and display joy by leaping and springing. As we obey God, He will bless the work of our hands. The Lord will make us successful in all that we do. That is an amazing promise, but what's more amazing than this is when we realize the Lord is so happy to bless us that He is leaping and springing in heaven!

> God loves to bless us so much that He's leaping and skipping in heaven.

During the days of Jeremiah, the people of Israel rebelled against God and worshipped other false gods. As a result, they were made prisoners and deported to Babylon. But Jeremiah prophesied that the day would come when the Lord *"will bring them back to this place and let them live in peace and safety. They shall be My people, and I will be their God. I will give them one heart and mind to worship Me forever, for their own good and for the good of all their descendants. I will make an everlasting covenant with them ...* **I will rejoice (i.e., suws) in doing them good** *and will faithfully plant them in this land with all My heart and all My soul ... I will also usher in a wonderful life of prosperity that I have promised them"* (Jer. 32:37, 41-42 NIV/NLT/NASB/MSG). Jeremiah echoes the promise Moses gave the Israelites years ago. The Lord rejoices (i.e., leaps and springs) in doing us good. God really enjoys blessing us!

We looked at this next verse earlier, but it is worth mentioning again. Isaiah said, *"[A]s a young man takes a virgin for his wife, so will your Maker be married to you;* **and as a husband has joy in his bride, so will the Lord your God rejoice (i.e., suws)** *and be happy with you"* (Isa. 62:5 BBE/NLT/MSG). The Lord rejoices over us as a bridegroom rejoices over his bride. See God leaping and springing all around you with happiness!

Isaiah concluded his book telling us the Lord will create a *"new heavens and a new earth ... **be glad and rejoice, twirl (i.e., giyl) forever**. For look I will create Jerusalem to be a delight, a rejoicing, a twirling (i.e., giyl) and her people a source of happiness"* (Isa. 65:17-18 NIV/NET/ERRB). When the Lord makes all things new, Jerusalem and her people will be a delight to the world. For God will make Jerusalem a *"place of twirling"* (Isa. 65:18 TLB/ERRB), a city of dancing. All creation will rejoice and join them by twirling and dancing with joy.

The Lord will dance. God says, *"**I will rejoice, twirl (i.e., giyl) over Jerusalem and take delight (i.e., suws) in My people;** the sound of weeping and crying will be heard in her no more"* (Isa. 65:19 NIV/NASB/ERRB). The Lord dances over His children! We know this, but it's worth repeating. The word for rejoice is *giyl* and means "to rejoice by spinning around, twirling, going in a circle, and leaping for joy as we dance." And the word for "take delight" is *suws*, which means "to rejoice by leaping and springing about." God is happy and knows how to show His joy over His people. Be like God and show your joy by dancing.

The Father Dances a War Dance as He Treads on Our Enemies

During a time when Israel turned away from the Lord, they suffered a defeat at the hand of their enemies. David stood in the gap and interceded for the nation. He asked God to forgive and restore them, to give Israel *"a **Father's help** when* *we face our enemies"* (Psa. 60:11 tPt). The Father responded to David's cry and acted!

*"God gave His sacred promise, 'I will rejoice, **jump for joy** (i.e., 'alaz). In My triumph, I will be the one to measure out the portion of My inheritance to My people, and I will secure the land as I promised you. Shechem, Succoth, Gilead, Manasseh, they are all still Mine!' He says, 'Judah will continue **to produce kings and lawgivers**, and Ephraim **will produce great warriors'"** (Psa. 60:6-7 ERRB/tPt). The Lord rejoiced and jumped for joy as He rescued His people and defeated their enemies.

God proclaimed His victory over Israel's adversaries, *"Moab is My scrub bucket; Upon Edom, I leave My sandal print; I shout (i.e., ruwa, a War Cry) in triumph over Philistia"* (Psa. 60:8 MSG/CW/NLT). The Lord made every adversary powerless before Him and His people.

The last eight verses of Psalm 60 contain God's promise of victory over Israel's enemies. They are so important that Holy Spirit has David repeat them later in Psalm 108. Once again, *"God gave His sacred promise; 'I will triumph, **I will rejoice, jump for joy** (i.e., 'alaz)'"* (Psa. 108:7 NET/ERRB/NKJV) as He restored the land of Israel as His inheritance and defeated their foes.

Both Psalms conclude with the battle cry, *"Through our God, we shall do valiantly; we will conquer [and] perform brave deeds as we fight victoriously like heroes. For it is He who shall **tread down** our enemies in the dust"* (Psa. 60:12, 108:13 NKJV/Har/Knox/NET/JB). Every Word God speaks is important, and when He repeats something, it means **"God establishes the thing, divinely settled and God will bring it to pass soon"** (Gen. 41:32 KJV/MLB). The Lord gave this promise twice (Psa. 60:5-12, 108:6-13) to show God establishes this revelation. The Lord gives a powerful image as we see Him dance a War Dance as He jumps for joy and tramples on our enemies in victory.

Years later, Paul repeats this vision in a powerful promise, *"And before you know it, the God of peace will come down on satan* **with both feet stomping him to the dirt***, swiftly pound satan to a pulp. Enjoy the best of Jesus, and the wonderful favor of our Lord Jesus surround you"* (Rom. 16:20 MSG/tPt). We receive God's peace and enjoy the best of Jesus as we watch the Father dance a War Dance. See God jump for joy, come down on satan with both feet, and pound him to a pulp. When the Lord Almighty jumps and lands on you with both feet, you're done.

WORSHIP THE FATHER SO DEEPLY THAT JESUS JOINS US

There's a beautiful verse in Hebrews where Jesus brags on everyone who has come to Him to be saved. Jesus *"is not ashamed to call them His brothers and sisters"* (Heb. 2:11 NLT). But then Jesus makes an amazing statement. *"He says, 'I will declare Your name to My brothers,* **in the midst of the church I will sing praise to You. I'll join them in worship and praise to You'"** (Heb. 2:12 NIV/KJV/MSG). One Bible version says Jesus *"will make a song of praise to You before the church"* (BBE). What an encouraging promise. Jesus will join us and praise the Father as we worship Father God!

I love to challenge worship leaders with this Word. I will ask them, "What is your goal in leading us in worship?" There should be a purpose in our praise, and it's not just to bless us and make us feel good. It's to honor and bless the Father, but there is more.

I challenge the worship leaders to bring us into such a deep level of worship that the Son tells the Father, "I have to join them in their worship and praise to You. I have to sing a song of praise to You in the midst of the church." Can you imagine this? We're praising the Father with all our hearts when suddenly *we hear the voice of Jesus joining us in worshipping Father God*! Can you imagine what that would sound like? I've heard testimonies of people who've heard the voice of Jesus join in their worship. What a glorious experience ... but it gets even better!

LET'S MAKE FATHER GOD SO HAPPY THAT HE WANTS TO DANCE

Not only do I challenge worship leaders to bring us to a point in worship where Jesus wants to join us, but also for them to bring us to the place where the Father wants to dance! The prophet Zephaniah tells God's people, *"The LORD has taken away the judgment against you.* **He has turned back your enemy.** *The King of Israel, the LORD is in your midst; you will fear disaster no more"* (Zeph. 3:15 NIV/NASB). The people of God rejoice because the Lord has driven away the enemy, and He now lives among them. "Yes, do that here, Lord, that we'll no longer fear disaster."

When we rejoice, God rejoices with us. Zephaniah says, *"The LORD your God is in your midst, a victorious Warrior mighty to save.* **He will rejoice (i.e., suws) over you with joy.** *He will quiet you in His love. With His love He will calm all your fears.* **He will exult, twirl (i.e., giyl) over you with shouts of joy,** *singing a happy song"* (Zeph. 3:17 NASB/NIV/NLT/ERRB). God will *leap and spring* over us with joy. The Lord will *spin around, go in a circle, and leap for joy* as He dances, shouts, and sings a happy song. Do we get the message that God is happy?

Here is my final challenge to worship leaders. Lead us into a level of praise and worship that causes the Father to keep time with our music with His fingers drumming on the armrest of His throne. Then He starts tapping His toes as He receives our worship. Then He can't stand it anymore; he jumps up and starts dancing on the dance floor of heaven!

The most blessed sight in the universe is seeing the Lord God of all creation, singing and dancing with joy over His children! See this in your spirit. Know that this will happen as we, with all our hearts, release our love to the Father. As this happens, we'll rejoice because everything is right in the world—Papa God is dancing tonight. "Dance, Papa, dance!"

> *Everything is right in the world; Papa is dancing tonight. Dance, Papa, dance!*

The Godhead Loves to Dance Over Us

The Father, Son, and Holy Ghost are three in one. They are the Godhead and move in unity. We have learned that Father God loves to dance and that Jesus the Son loves to dance. What about the Holy Spirit? He is one with the Father and Son, so that means He loves to dance too. But ask yourself, how does the Holy Ghost dance? He dances through us!

The Holy Ghost gets to dance when we dance. As the Body of Christ, we have the honor and privilege to bless the Holy Spirit when we dance. Because when we dance, Holy Ghost gets his chance to dance too!

One work of the Holy Spirit is to honor the Father and the Son. So as the Father and Son dance with joy over us, the Holy Spirit can respond back to Them when we allow Him to dance through us. What an honor, what a privilege, what a joy!

When it's all said and done, we're all going to be one big, happy, War Dancing family.

> The Holy Spirit loves to dance, and we have the honor to allow Him to dance through us!

ENDNOTES

1. The Hebrew word *bazah* is Strong's H595 at: www.blbclassic.org/lang/lexicon/Lexicon.cfm?Strongs=H959&t=KJV .
2. Seekins, p. 10.

Conclusion

Everybody Dance a War Dance Now!

Praise Him with drums and dancing.
Praise Him every instrument you can find.
Let everything that has breath praise the Lord.

Psa. 150:4-6 tPt/NIV

A War Dancing Church is a Victorious Church

Satan hates a dancing Church. It's dangerous to him. Dancing is a spiritual weapon. It releases the joy of the Lord, which along with *"righteousness and peace,"* are the foundation of God's Kingdom (Rom. 14:17). *"Joy in the Holy Spirit"* releases God's strength. As a result, a War Dancing Church is a strong Church that cannot be defeated as it advances the Kingdom of God.

At the beginning of the Twentieth Century, the Holy Spirit fell and refreshed the Church in a fresh baptism of the Holy Spirit and speaking in tongues. In the same way, the Holy Spirit is moving now, and this century will be known as *The Age of the War Dancing Church*. The Lord's War Dances will have the same impact on empowering the Church as the baptism in the Spirit and praying in tongues did.

This century will be more powerful because we'll add singing War Songs, shouting War Cries, waving War Flags, blowing War Horns, and playing musical weapons with many other spiritual weapons as we dance our War Dances. We love it when the God of peace crushes satan under our feet (Rom. 16:20), but we really enjoy it when we get to dance on the devil's head as He crushes him.

IT'S TIME TO DANCE AND LAUGH AT THE LAST DAYS

Now is the season for the warriors of God to dance, not just dances of love, but dances of war. We need to bring the battle to the gates of hell and smash them with God's musical weapons as we play His War Songs and dance the War Dances of God.

At the first notes of our praise, the Lord strikes the kingdom of darkness. *"As soon as they started shouting and praising, the Lord caused great confusion in the enemy camp. God turned the ambushes of them against themselves, the people of Ammon, Moab, and Edom who had come to attack Judah. They were utterly defeated, turning on one another, fighting among themselves, and all ended up dead"* (2 Chron. 20:22-24 MSG/CEV/Voice/WYC/NCV/TLB). There was so much plunder it took Israel three days to gather the spoils of war, and *"on the fourth day, they assembled in the*

Valley of Berachah, where they praised the Lord. That is why the valley is called **the Valley of Praise**" (2 Chron. 20:25-26 CW/NET). What a powerful revelation of what happens in the spiritual arena when we enter into warfare-worship! This is why we can dance and laugh at the future. Wherever we assemble, we transform that place into a place of praise.

As the Bride of Christ, as God's mighty women of valor, no matter what is going on, we can laugh at the future. We have no fear of winter because our family is *"clothed with scarlet"* (Prov. 31:25 KJV). We are all covered by the blood of the Lamb. As Jesus' Bride, we are clothed with strength and honor; we *"can laugh with no fear at the future"* (Prov. 31:25 NIV/NLT). When we *"think about the future,"* we can *"laugh with joy at the latter days"* (Voice/tPt/RSV). Don't listen to the fear-mongers. The Word says because we walk with Jesus, we have no fear of the last days.

The Hebrew word for laugh is *sachaq* (pronounced saw-hak) and means "to laugh, mock, to make sport of, and to play (including musical instruments, singing, and dancing)."[1] We have studied this word earlier, but here is how *sachaq* is translated when it is describing David's dancing (1 Chron. 15:29) in a few Bible versions:

- *"leaping in sport"* (Amp),
- *"dancing"* (CEB),
- *"leaping for joy"* (GNT),
- *"playing music"* (NKJV),
- *"cavorting around"* (ISV),
- *"spinning"* (MEV),
- and *"whirling"* (OJB).

If you ask some believers how they feel when they think about the last days, too many answers are filled with fear. This is wrong! Who are they listening to? It's not God and His Word.

The Proverbs 31 woman reflects the Bride of Christ. Like her, we laugh at the latter days. Like David, when we think about the last days, we *sachaq*! We leap for joy, dance, spin, whirl, and cavort all over the place. God says this is what we do whenever we think about the future. Why? Because as the Warrior Bride of Jesus, we know He has defeated sin, death, and the devil. We know that nothing can separate us from His love (Rom. 8:39 KJV), and *"in all these things we are more than conquerors through Him who loved us"* (Rom. 8:37 KJV). So, who or what shall we fear!

> When the Bride of Christ thinks about the last days, she laughs and dances.

This is the Age of the New Covenant: The Time to Dance

Jeremiah prophecies and says, "'*The days are coming,*' declares the Lord, '*when* **I will make a new covenant** *with the people of Israel and the people of Judah ...* **I will be their God, and they will be My people**'" (Jer. 31:31, 33b NIV). Those days have arrived, and the Lord says His people will dance!

The Lord says, "*I will rebuild you, My virgin Israel so that you will once again be built up. Once again you will take up the tambourine* **and go out in the round dance** *(i.e., machowl) with those who rejoice (i.e., sachaq)*" (Jer. 31:4 NET/NLT/NIV/NKJV/ERRB). We'll dance (i.e., *machowl*) our round dance as we whirl, spin, and go in a circle with those who rejoice (i.e., *sachaq*) who laugh, mock, play, and dance. Again, God says, *"At that time the virgin will rejoice in the round dance (i.e., machowl) ... For I will convert their weeping into laughter, lavishing comfort, invading their grief with joy"* (Jer. 31:13 NET/NASB/MSG/ERRB). The New Covenant age is the time of God's joy, laughter, and comfort. This is the age of the War Dancing Church!

Jeremiah said the day would come when the Lord would return the Jews to the land of Israel, where they would live in safety (Jer. 32:37). That day started in 1948, and the people of God are still returning to their homeland. During this time of return and restoration, the Lord says, *"They will be My people, and I will be their God. And I will give them one heart and mind to worship Me forever ... I will make an everlasting covenant with them that I will not turn away from them, to do them good; and I will put the fear of Me in their hearts so that they will not turn away from Me. Oh how I'll rejoice (i.e., suws) over them! Oh, how I'll delight in doing good things for them! Heart and soul, I'll plant then in this country and keep them here"* (Jer. 32:38, 41 NIV/ NLT/ NASB/MSG). This age of Israel's restoration is the day God rejoices by leaping and springing all around them. It is the day of the Lord's everlasting covenant when God dances. This is why the people of God are dancing too!

The 21st Century is the Century of the War Dancing Church

The Lord is using the first decade of the 2020s to usher in what He desires for the Twenty-First Century. In the 1920s, we had *the world's* roaring 20s. Now a hundred years later, in the 2020s, we're going to experience *the Lord's* roaring 20s! As the Bride of Christ, we will not just dance; we will dance War Dances! The 21st century will be known as the Age of the War Dancing Church.

The 1920s were the world's roaring 20s. The 2020s will be the Lord's roaring 20s!

Here are a few verses where we are told to rejoice (i.e., *giyl*) by dancing, by going in a circle, spinning around, and leaping for joy.

- Dance for *"the Lord reigns as King"* (1 Chron. 16:31).
- Dance and rejoice in God's *"salvation"* (Psa. 9:14).
- Dance for the Lord has *"delivered us from captivity"* (Psa. 14:7).
- Dance and rejoice in God's *"mercy"* (Psa. 31:7).
- Dance as God's *"light and truth lead us to His Temple"* (Psa. 43:3-4).
- Dance as we *"enter into the King's palace"* (Psa. 45:15).
- Dance and rejoice for God's *"judgment"* on the wicked (Psa. 97:8-10).
- Dance and rejoice in God's *"harvest"* (Isa. 9:3).
- Dance and rejoice in *"the Holy One of Israel"* (Isa. 29:19).
- Dance and rejoice in God's *"glory and excellency"* (Isa. 35:2).
- Dance and rejoice in God's *"comfort and compassion"* (Isa. 49:13).

- Dance for God has clothed us with *"a robe of righteousness"* (Isa. 61:10).

- Dance and rejoice over *"Jerusalem and God's people"* (Isa. 65:18).

- Dance and rejoice for God *"will do great things"* (Joel 2:21).

- Dance for God will *"give us the former and latter rain"* (Joel 2:23).

- Dance with God as He *"dances over us with joy and singing"* (Zeph. 3:17).

- Dance because when our children see us dancing, they will join us and *"dance in the Lord"* (Zech. 10:7)

We need to dance and thank God each morning. For *"this is the day the Lord has made, **we will rejoice, twirl (i.e., giyl) and be glad in it"*** (Psa. 118:24 KJV/ERRB). God tells us to dance every day. Why, so He can pour out all these blessings upon His children!

The Praise Band and Worshippers are the Warriors in God's Army

In conclusion: I encourage you by reminding you that God's praise band is His Army. Don't see them as a group of musicians playing musical instruments. Instead of holding a guitar, they are holding God's bow. As they play, they are pulling back God's bow and releasing His arrows of glory. Instead of flutes and pipes, see them holding God's dart gun and blowing His darts of fire into the camp of the wicked one. They pierce the darkness with God's light. Instead of just beating a drum, see God keep time with the drummers and His Word like a club pounds on the eneny's head to the rhythm of their drums.

God the Father loves to dance. Jesus the Son loves to dance. The Holy Ghost loves to dance and wants to dance! Bless the Holy Spirit by allowing Him to dance through you.

All around God's musical Army are His worshippers, His dancing Warriors. We celebrate dancing God's War Dances. We dance *before* the battle as a confession of our faith in the Lord's victory. We dance our War Dance *during* the battle because that is sometimes how we fight. And we definitely dance *after* the battle to celebrate the triumph of Jesus our Lord and Savior. So, dance, Warriors of God, dance!

Dance, Warriors of God, dance!

ENDNOTE

1. The Hebrew word *sachaq* is Strong's H7832 at: http://www.blbclassic.org/lang/lexicon/lexicon.cfm?Strongs=H7832&t=KJV.

APPENDIX

List of Bible Translations and Abbreviations

Throughout this book, I have used wording from many translations, combining them for clearer understanding. I have denoted all the versions used following each reference, even though it may only have been a few words. Many people paraphrase scripture, and some may criticize my approach as trying to manipulate words or make the verses say what I want them to say to back up my concepts.

Nothing could be further from the truth. I honor God's Word. I appreciate the thought and labor that has gone into each translation—knowing that every word was painstakingly considered, compared, and thoughtfully chosen. It is this respect that drives me to be so careful in citing source material. The list below is my best effort to provide accurate copyright information and give proper credit to publishers and authors alike. I invite you to look into these resources and study them for yourself. The richness of the language of the Bible is a beautiful thing!

James M. Massa
September, 2021

- **AAT – An American Translation**
  Portions of scripture taken from *The Holy Bible in the Language of Today, AN AMERICAN TRANSLATION* are marked AAT. William F. Beck. Copyright © by William F. Beck. A.J. Holman Company. Philadelphia, PA,

- **AB – Aramaic Bible**
  Portions of scripture taken from the *Aramaic Bible* are marked AB. Vic Alexander. Burbank, CA. Retrieved at: http://www.v-a.com/bible.

- **ABPS – American Baptist Publication Sociey**
  Portions of scripture taken from the *Holy Bible Containing the Old and New Testament: An Improved Edition* (American Baptist Publication Society) are marked ABPS. Retrieved from *The WORD: The Bible From 26 Translations.* Copyright © 1988, © 1991, © 1993 Mathis Publishers, Inc., Moss Point, MS: 1993. All rights reserved.

- **ABUV – Amercian Bible Union Version**
  Portions of scripture taken from *The New Testament of Our Lord and Savior Jesus Christ,* American Bible Union Version by John A. Broadus et al are marked ABUV. United Bible Society. Retrieved from *The WORD: The Bible From 26 Translations.* Copyright © 1988, © 1991, © 1993 Mathis Publishers, Inc., Moss Point, MS: 1993. All rights reserved.

- **AEB – (2001 Translation) An American English Bible**
  Portions of scripture taken from *An American English Bible* are marked AEB. Jim Wheeler, Editor. Retrieved at: http://www.2001translation.com.

- **AMP – Amplifed® Bible**
  Portions of scripture taken from the *Amplifed® Bible* are marked AMP. Copyright © 1954, 1958, 1962, 1964, 1965, 1987 by The Lockman Foundation. Used by permission. www.lockman.org

- **ARTB – Ancient Roots Translinear Bible**
  Portions of scripture taken from the *Ancient Roots Translinear Bible* are marked ARTB. A. Francis Werner. Copyright © 2005, 2006. Used by permission of the author."

- **ASV – American Standard Version**
  Portions of scripture taken from the *American Standard Version* are marked ASV. This Bible is in the public domain. © 1901.

- **BBE – The Bible in Basic English**
  Portions of scripture taken from the *The Bible in Basic English* are marked BBE. C. K. Ogden. New York, NY: Cambridge University Press, (© date unavailable).

- **Beck – The Holy Bible in the Language of Today: An American Translation**
  Portions of scripture taken from *The Holy Bible in the Language of Today: An American Translation* by William F. Beck are marked Beck. Copyright © 1976 by Mrs. William F. Beck. Jointly published by A. J. Holman Company, division of J. B. Lippincott Company and Leader Press, New York: 1978. All rights reserved.

- **CAB – The Complete Apostles Bible**
  Portions of scripture taken from *The Complete Apostles Bible* are marked CAB. Paul W. Esposito; *The Complete Apostles' Bible*. Paul W. Esposito, ed. Bloomington, IL: Authorhouse, © 2005.

- **CBW – The New Testament: A Translation in the Language of the People**
  Portions of scripture taken from *The New Testament: A Translation in the Language of the People* by Charles B. Williams are marked CBW. Moody Bible Institute. Copyright © 1937 by Bruce Humphries, Inc. Moody Press, Chicago: 1955. All rights reserved.

- **CCB – Christian Community Bible 2nd Edition**
  Portions of scripture taken from the *Christian Community Bible 2nd Edition* are marked CCB. Bernardo Hurault © 1988; *Christian Community Bible, 2nd Edition*. Bernardo Hurault. Madrid, Spain: San Pablo Internacional and Editorial Verbo Divino,

- **CEB – Common English Bible**
  Portions of scripture taken from the *Common English Bible* are marked CEB. Copyright © 2011 by Common English Bible. Retrieved from http://www.commonenglishbible.com.

- **CEV –** *Contemporary English Version*
  Portions of scripture taken from the *Contemporary English Bible* are marked CEV. Copyright © 1995 by American Bible Society; *The Promise: Contemporary English Version*. Nashville, TN: Thomas Nelson Publishers, 1995.

- **CJB – Complete Jewish Bible**
  Portions of scripture taken from the *Complete Jewish Bible* are marked CJB. Copyright © 1998 by David H. Stern. Jewish New Testament Publications, Inc. Clarksville, MD.

- **Con - The Epistles of Paul**
  Portions of scripture taken from The Epistles of Paul by W. J. Conybeare are marked Con. Baker Book House. Retrieved from The WORD: The Bible From 26 Translations. Copyright © 1988, 1991, 1993 Mathis Publishers, Inc., Moss Point, MS: 1993. All rights reserved.

- **CTB – The Combined Translations Bible**
  Portions of scripture taken from *The Combined Translations Bible* are marked CTB (*work in progress*).

- **CV – Confraternity Version of The Old Testament**
  Portions of scripture taken from the *Confraternity of Christian Doctrine Translation; The Old Testament of the Holy Bible: Confraternity Version* are marked CV. Copyright © 1964 by Joseph A. Grispino. New York, NY: Guild Press.

- **CW – The Clear Word**
  Portions of scripture taken from *The Clear Word* are marked CW. Paraphrased by Jack J. Blanco; Copyright © 2003 by Jack J. Blanco All rights reserved. Hagerstown, MD.

- **Dar – Darby Translation**
  Portions of scripture taken from the *Darby Translation* are marked Dar. This Bible is in the public domain.

- **DeW – Praise-Songs of Israel: A Rendering of the Book of Psalms**
  Portions of scripture taken from *Praise-Songs of Israel: A Rendering of the Book of Psalms* by John DeWitt are marked DeW. Retrieved from *The WORD: The Bible From 26 Translations*. Copyright © 1988, 1991, 1993 Mathis Publishers, Inc., Moss Point, MS: 1993. All rights reserved.

- **DRB – Douay-Rheims 1899 American Edition.**
  Portions of scripture taken from the *Douay-Rheims © 1899 American Edition* are marked DRB. This Bible is in the public domain.

- **ERRB – Exegeses Ready Research Bible™**
  Portions of scripture taken from the *Second Edition: Exegeses Ready Research Bible* are marked ERRB. Copyright (C) 1993 by Herb Jahn, Exegete. Used by permission of World Bible Publishers, Iowa Falls, IA. All rights reserved.

- **ERV – Holy Bible: Easy-to-Read Version**
  Portions of scripture taken from the *Holy Bible: Easy to Read Version*™ are marked ERV. Copyright © 2006 by World Bible Translation Center, Inc. and used by permission.

- **ESV – English Standard Version**
  Portions of scripture taken from the *English Standard Version* are marked ESV. Copyright © 2001 by Crossway Bibles, a division of Good News Publishers. Used by permission. All rights reserved.

- **EXB – The Expanded Bible**
  Portions of scripture taken from *The Expanded Bible* are marked EXB. Copyright © 2011 by Thomas Nelson, Inc. Used by permission. All rights reserved.

- **GNB – Good News Bible**
  (also known as Today's English Version – TEV)
  Portions of scripture taken from the *Good News Bible: The Bible in Today's English Version* are marked GNB. Copyright © 1976 by the American Bible Society. New York, NY.

- **GNT – Good News Translation**
  Portions of scripture taken from the *Good News Translation, Second Edition, Today's English Version* are marked GNT. Copyright © 1992 by American Bible Society. Used by permission. All rights reserved.

- **GOD'S WORD – God's Word Translation**
  Portions of scripture taken from *God's Word Translation* are marked GOD'S WORD. GOD'S WORD is a copyrighted work of God's Word to the Nations Bible Society. Quotations are used by permission. Copyright © 1995 by God's Word to the Nations. All rights reserved.

- **Gspd – The New Testament: An American Translation**
  Portions of scripture taken from *The New Testament: An American Translation* by Edgar J. Goodspeed are marked Gspd. Copyright © 1923, 1948 by the University of Chicago Press. Retrieved from *The WORD: The Bible From 26 Translations*. Copyright © 1988, © 1991, © 1993 Mathis Publishers, Inc., Moss Point, MS: 1993. All rights reserved.

- **Har – The Psalms for Today: A New Translation from the Hebrew into Current English**
  Portions of scripture taken from *The Psalms for Today: A New Translation from the Hebrew into Current English* by R. K. Harrison are marked Har. Retrieved from *The WORD: The Bible From 26 Translations*. Copyright © 1988, © 1991, © 1993 Mathis Publishers, Inc., Moss Point, MS: 1993. All rights reserved.

- **HCSB – Holman Cristian Standard Bible**
  Portions of scripture taken from the *Holman Christian Standard Bible* are marked HCSB. Copyright © 1999, 2000, 2002, 2003 by Holman Bible Publishers. All rights reserved.

- **HNV – Hebrew Names Version**
  (also known as World English Bible – WEB)
  Portions of scripture taken from the *Hebrew Names Version* are marked HNV. This Bible is in the public domain.

- **ISR – The Scriptures**
  Portions of scripture taken from *The Scriptures* are marked ISR. Copyright © 2010 by Institute for Scriptural Research. South Africa. All rights reserved.

- **ISV – International Standard Version**
  Portions of scripture taken from the *International Standard Version* are marked ISV. Copyright © 1995-2014 by ISV Foundation. All Rights Reserved Internationally. Used by permission of Davidson Press, LLC.

- **JB – The Jerusalem Bible**
  Portions of scripture taken from *The Jerusalem Bible* are marked JB. The Jerusalem Bible. Alexander Jones, General Editor. Copyright © 1966 by Darton, Longmann & Todd, Ltd. and Doubleday & Company, Inc. Garden City, NY. All rights rights reserved.

- **JPS - The Jewish Publication Society**
  Portions of scripture taken from *The Holy Scriptures According to the Masoretic Texts: A New Translation* are marked JPS. Copyright © 1955 by the Jewish Publication Society of America. All rights reserved.

- **JUB – Jubilee Bible**
  Portions of scripture taken from the *Jubilee Bible* are marked JUB. The Jubilee Bible © 2000, 2000, 2001, 2010 by LIFE SENTENCE Publishing. All rights reserved.

- **KJV – King James Version**
  Portions of scripture taken from the *King James Version* are marked KJV. Originally published in 1611, this Bible is in the public domain.

- **Knox – Knox Bible: The Holy Bible, A Translation from the Latin Vulgate in the light of the Hebrew and Greek Originals**
  Portions of scripture taken from the *Knox Bible* are marked Knox. Monsignor Ronald Knox. Copyright © 1961 by Burns and Oates, London, England. Copyright pertains to all countries which are signatories to the Berne Convention.

- **Lam – The Holy Bible From The Ancient Eastern Texts**
  Portions of scripture taken from *The Holy Bible From The Ancient Eastern Texts,* George M. Lamsa's Translation From the Aramaic of the Peshitta are marked Lam. Copyright © 1940, 1957, 1961 by A. J. Holman Company. Harper, San Francisco: 1961. All rights reserved.

- **LEB – Lexham® English Bible**
  Portions of scripture taken from the *Lexham English Bible* are marked LEB. Copyright © 2012 by Logos Bible Software. Lexham is a registered trademark of Logos Bible Software.

- **MLB – The Modern Language Bible**
  Portions of scripture taken from *The Modern Language Bible* iare marked MLB. The New Berkeley Version. Gerrit Verkuyl, Editor-in-Chief. Copyright © 1945, 1959, 1969, 1971 by Zondervan Publishing House. Grand Rapids, MI.

- **Mof – A New Translation of the Bible**
  Portions of scripture taken from *A New Translation of the Bible* are marked Mof. James A. Moffatt, Editor. Copyright © 1972 Harper & Row Publishers New York, NY.

- **Mont – The New Testament in Modern English**
  Portions of scripture taken from *The New Testament in Modern English* translated by Helen Barrett Montgomery are marked Mont. Copyright © 1924 by Judson Press, Valley Forge, PA. Used by permission. Holman Bible Publishers, Nashville: 1988. All rights reserved.

- **Mounce – Mounce Reverse-Interlinear™ New Testament**
  Portions of scripture taken from the *Mounce Reverse-Interlinear™ New Testament* are marked Mounce. Copyright © 2011 by Robert H Mounce and William D Mounce. Used by permission. All rights reserved worldwide.

- **MRB – The Modern Reader's Bible**
  Portions of scripture taken from *The Modern Reader's Bible* are marked MRB. Richard G. Moulton Copyright © 1895, 1896, 1897, 1898, 1899, 1907, 1923, 924, 1925, 1926, 1927, and 1935. by Macmillan Co. New York, NY.

- **MSG – The Message**
  Portions of scripture taken from the *THE MESSAGE* are marked MSG. by Eugene H. Peterson. Copyright © 1993, 1994, 1995, 1996, 2000, 2001, 2002. Used by permission of NavPress Publishing Group.

- **NAB – New American Bible**
  Portions of scripture taken from the *New American Bible* are marked NAB. The text of the *New American Bible* is reproduced by license of Confraternity of Christian Doctrine, Washington, D.C.; the owner of said Bible. Copyright © 1970 by P.J. Kenedy & Sons, New York, NY. All rights reserved.

- **NABRE – The New American Bible Revised Edition**
  Portions of scripture taken from *The New American Bible Revised Edition* are marked NABRE. Copyright © 2011 Good Will Publishers, Inc. Saint Benedict Press, LLC, Charlotte, NC: 2011. All rights reserved.

- **NASB – New American Standard Bible**
  Portions of scripture taken from the *New American Standard Bible* are marked NASB. Copyright © 1960, 1962, 1963, 1968, 1971, 1972, 1973, 1975, 1977, 1995 by The Lockman Foundation. Used by permission.

- **NCV – New Century Version**
  Portions of scripture taken from the *The Holy Bible, New Century Version*® are marked NCV. Copyright © 1987, 1988, 1991, by Word Publishing, Dallas, TX. Used by permission.

- **NEB – The New English Bible**
  Portions of scripture taken from *The New English Bible* are marked NEB. Donald Ebor, Chairman. Copyright © 1974 by Cambridge University Press. Oxford, England.

- **NET – New English Translation**
  Portions of scripture taken from the *New English Translation (The NET Bible*®*)* are designated NET. Scripture quoted by permission. Copyright © 1996-2006 by Biblical Studies Press. All rights reserved.

- **NETS – New English Translation of the Septuagint**
  Portions of scripture taken from the *New English Translation of the Septuagint* are marked NETS. Pietersma & Wright. Copyright © 2007 by the International Organization for Septuagint and Cognate Studies, Inc. Used by permission of Oxford University Press. All rights reserved.

- **NIRV – New International Reader's Version**
  Portions of scripture taken from the *New International Reader's Version*® are marked NIRV. Copyright © 1995, 1996, 1998 by International Bible Society. Used by permission of Zondervan. All rights reserved.

- **NIV – New International Version**
  Portions of scripture taken from the *Holy Bible, New International Version*®, NIV® are marked NIV. Copyright © 1973, 1978, 1984 by the International Bible Society. Used by permission of Zondervan Publishing House. All rights reserved. The "NIV" and "New International Version" are trademarks registered in the United States Patent and Trademark Office by the International Bible Society. Use of either trademark requires the permission of the International Bible Society.

- **NIVUK – New International Version: UK**
  Portions of scripture taken from the *Holy Bible, New International Version*® *Anglicized, NIV*® are marked NIVUK. Copyright © 1979, 1984, 2011 by Biblica, Inc.® Used by permission. All rights reserved worldwide.

- **NJB – New Jerusalem Bible**
  Portions of scripture taken from the *New Jerusalem Bible* are marked NJB. Copyright © 1999 by Doubleday, a division of Random House, Inc., and Darton, Longman & Todd Ltd. New York, NY.

- **NKJV – New King James Version**
  Portions of scripture taken from the *New King James Version* are marked NKJV. Copyright © 1979, 1980, 1982 by Thomas Nelson, Inc. Used by permission. All rights reserved.

- **NLT – New Living Translation**
  Portions of scripture taken from *The Holy Bible, New Living Translation* are marked NLT. Copyright © 1996. Used by permission by Tyndale House Publishers, Inc., Wheaton, IL. All rights reserved.

- **NLV – New Life Version**
  Portions of scripture taken from the *Holy Bible, New Life Version* are marked NLV. Copyright © 1969 – 2003 by Christian Literature International, Canby, OR. Used by permission.

- **Noli – The New Testament of our Lord and Savior Jesus Christ**
  Portions of scripture taken from *The New Testament of our Lord and Savior Jesus Christ by* Metropolitan Fan S. Noli are marked Noli. Copyright © 1961 Albanian Orthodox Church in America, Boston. Website at http://www.albanianorthodox.com/tekste/liturgjike/Noli_1961.pdf.

- **Norlie – The New Testament: A New Translation**
  Portions of scripture taken from *The New Testament: A New Translation* by Olaf M. Norlie are marked Norlie. Copyright © 1961 by Zondervan Publishing House. Retrieved from *The WORD: The Bible From 26 Translations*. Copyright © 1988, © 1991, © 1993 Mathis Publishers, Inc., Moss Point, MS: 1993. All rights reserved.

- **NRSV – New Revised Standard Version**
  Portions of scripture taken from the *New Revised Version Bible* are marked NRSV. Copyright © 1989 the Division of Christian Education of the National Council of the Churches of Christ in the United States of America. Used by permission. All rights reserved.

- **NTPE – The New Testament: A New Translation in Plain English**
  Portions of scripture taken from *The New Testament: A New Translation in Plain English* are marked NTPE. Charles Kingsley Williams. Copyright © 1952 by Longman, Green & Co, University Press, Cambridge.

- **OJB – Orthodox Jewish Bible**
  Portions of scripture taken from the *Orthodox Jewish Bible* are marked OJB. Copyright © 2002, 2003, 2008, 2010 by Artists for Israel International. All rights reserved.

- **OSB – Orthodox Study Bible**
  Portions of scripture taken from the *Orthodox Study Bible* are marked OSB. Copyright © 2008 prepared under the auspices of the academic community of St. Athanasius Academy of Orthodox Theology, Elk Grove, California. *The Orthodox Study Bible*. Thomas Nelson. All Rights Reserved.

- **PBV – The Psalms in the Book of Common Prayer by the Anglican Church**
  Portions of scripture taken from *The Psalms in the Book of Common Prayer by the Anglican Church* are marked PBV. Retrieved from *The WORD: The Bible From 26 Translations*. Copyright © 1988, © 1991, © 1993 Mathis Publishers, Inc., Moss Point, MS: 1993. All rights reserved.

- **Phi – Four Prophets Amos, Hosea, First Isaiah, Micah: A Modern Translation from the Hebrew**
  Portions of scripture taken from the *Four Prophets Amos, Hosea, First Isaiah: Micah: A Modern Translation from Hebrew* are marked Phi. J. B. Phillips. Copyright © 1963 by The Macmillan Company. New York, NY.

- **PHILLIPS – J. B. Phillips New Testament**
  Portions of Scripture taken from the *J.B. Phillips New Testament, The New Testament in Mondern English* are marked PHILLIPS. Copyright © 1960, 1972 J.B. Phillips. Administered by The Archbishop's Council of the Church of Englad. Used by permission.

- **REB – The Revised English Bible**
  Portions of scripture taken from *The Revised English Bible* are marked REB. Copyright © 1989. Revision of the New English Bible Oxford, Cambridge Press.

APPENDIX | 171

- **Rhm – The Emphasized Bible**
  Portions of scripture taken from *The Emphasized Bible* are marked Rhm. Joseph Bryant Rotherham. Copyright © 1959, 1994 by Kregel Publications. Grand Rapids, MI.

- **Rieu – The Four Gospels**
  Portions of scripture taken from *The Four Gospels* translated by E. V. Rieu is marked Rieu. Copyright © 1957 by Penguin Press, Ltd. Portions of scripture taken from *The Acts of the Apostles* translated by C. H. Rieu are marked Rieu. Copyright © 1957 by C. H. Rieu. Retrieved from *The WORD: The Bible From 26 Translations*. Copyright © 1988, © 1991, © 1993 Mathis Publishers, Inc., Moss Point, MS: 1993. All rights reserved.

- **RSV – Revised Standard Version**
  Portions of scripture taken from the *Revised Standard Version* are marked RSV. Copyright © 1946, 1952, and 1971 by the Division of Christian Education of the National Council of the Churches of Christ in the United States of America. Used by permission All rights reserved;

- **Sept – The Holy Bible from the Greek (Septuagint)**
  Portions of scripture taken from *The Holy Bible from the Greek (Septuagint)* are marked Sept. Charles Thompson, J. Aitken, PA. Retrieved at: http://thetencommandmentsministry.us/ministry/charlesthompson_thompson.

- **Sprl – A Translation of the Old Testament Scriptures From the Original Hebrew**
  Portions of scripture taken from *A Translation of the Old Testament Scriptures From the Original Hebrew* by Helen Spurrell are marked Sprl. Retrieved from *The WORD: The Bible From 26 Translations*. Copyright © 1988, © 1991, © 1993 Mathis Publishers, Inc., Moss Point, MS: 1993. All rights reserved.

- **TCNT – The Twentieth Century New Testament**
  Portions of scripture taken from *The Twentieth Century New Testament* are marked TCNT. Moody Bible Institute. Retrieved from *The WORD: The Bible From 26 Translations*. Copyright © 1988, © 1991, © 1993 Mathis Publishers, Inc., Moss Point, MS: 1993. All rights reserved.

- **TLB – The Living Bible**
  Portions of scripture taken from *The Living Bible* are marked TLB. Kenneth N. Taylor. Copyright © 1971. Used by permission of Tyndale House Publishers, Inc., Wheaton, IL. All rights reserved.

- **TLV – Tree of Life Version**
  Portions of scripture taken from the *Tree of Life Version* are marked TLV. *Tree of Life Translation of the Bible.* Copyright © 2015 by The Messianic Jewish Family Bible Society.

- **TNIV – Today's New International Version**
  Portions of scripture taken from *Today's New International Version*® are marked TNIV. Copyright © 2001, 2005 by International Bible Society®. All rights reserved.

- **Tor – The Torah: The Five Books of Moses**
  Portions of scripture taken from *The Torah: The Five Books of Moses* are marked Tor. Copyright © 1955 by The Jewish Publication Society of America. Retrieved from *The WORD: The Bible From 26 Translations.* Copyright © 1988, © 1991, © 1993 Mathis Publishers, Inc., Moss Point, MS: 1993. All rights reserved.

- **tPt — The Passion Translation**
  - Scripture quotations marked tPt are taken from *The Psalms: Poetry on Fire, The Passion Translation*®, copyright © 2014. Used by permission of Broadstreet Publishing Group, LLC, Racine, Wisconsin, USA. All rights reserved.

  - Scripture quotations marked tPt are taken from *Matthew: Our Loving King, The Passion Translation*®, copyright © 2014. Used by permission of Broadstreet Publishing Group, LLC, Racine, Wisconsin, USA. All rights reserved.

  - Scripture quotations marked tPt are taken from *Mark: Miracles and Mercy, The Passion Translation*®, copyright © 2014. Used by permission of Broadstreet Publishing Group, LLC, Racine, Wisconsin, USA. All rights reserved.

APPENDIX | 173

- Scripture quotations marked tPt are taken from *Luke and Acts: To the Lovers of God, The Passion Translation®*, copyright © 2014. Used by permission of Broadstreet Publishing Group, LLC, Racine, Wisconsin, USA. All rights reserved.

- Scripture quotations marked tPt are taken from *John: Eternal Love, The Passion Translation®*, copyright © 2014. Used by permission of Broadstreet Publishing Group, LLC, Racine, Wisconsin, USA. All rights reserved.

- Scripture quotations marked tPt are taken from *Romans: Grace and Glory, The Passion Translation®*, copyright © 2015. Used by permission of Broadstreet Publishing Group, LLC, Racine, Wisconsin, USA. All rights reserved.

- Scripture quotations marked tPt are taken from *1 & 2 Corinthians: Love and Truth, The Passion Translation®*, copyright © 2014. Used by permission of Broadstreet Publishing Group, LLC, Racine, Wisconsin, USA. All rights reserved.

- Scripture quotations marked tPt are taken from *Letters from Heaven by the Apostle Paul, The Passion Translation®*, copyright © 2014. Used by permission of Broadstreet Publishing Group, LLC, Racine, Wisconsin, USA. All rights reserved.

- Scripture quotations marked tPt are taken from *Hebrews and James: Faith Works, The Passion Translation®*, copyright © 2014. Used by permission of Broadstreet Publishing Group, LLC, Racine, Wisconsin, USA. All rights reserved.

- **Voice – The Voice Bible**
Portions of scripture taken from *The Voice™ Bible* are marked Voice. Copyright © 2012 by Thomas Nelson, Inc. Ecclesia Bible Society.

- **Vul – Latin Vulgate Text, English Translation**
  Portions of scripture taken from the *Latin Vulgate Text, English Translation (CPDV), and Translation Commentary,* Robert L. Conte Jr., translator and editor are marked Vul. Retrieved at http://www.sacredbible.org/studybible/.

- **WEB – World English Bible**
  Portions of scripture taken from the *World English Bible*™ are marked WEB. This Bible is in the public domain.

- **Wey – The New Testament in Modern Speech**
  Portions of scripture taken from *The New Testament in Modern Speech* are marked Wey. Copyright © 1944 by Richard Francis Weymouth. The Pilgrim Press, Boston.

- **Wuest – The New Testament an Expanded Version**
  Portions of scripture taken from *The New Testament an Expanded Version* are marked Wuest. Kenneth S. Wuest. Copyright © 2012 by William B. Eerdmans Publishing Company. Grand Rapids, MI.

- **WYC – Wycliff Bible**
  Portions of scripture taken from the *Wycliff Bible* are marked WYC. Copyright © 2001 by Terence P. Noble. Retrieved at http://www.ibiblio.org.

- **YLT – Young's Literal Translation**
  Portions of scripture taken from the *Young's Literal Translation* are marked YLT. This Bible is in the public domain.

Meet the Author

James "Mark" Massa

James M. Massa is a retired Lieutenant Colonel with thirty years in the military—a veteran of both the Vietnam War and the War on Terror. He served six years with the U.S. Marines and 24 years with the U.S. Air Force. His last five years in the Air Force (2008-2012) were spent serving as the Chief Nurse in the 118th Medical Group of the 118th Airlift Wing in Nashville, TN.

Massa's service in the Marines taught him the importance of knowing his weapons and how to fight. His service in the Air Force medical field taught him the importance of knowing how to heal those who were wounded in the fight.

This military background coupled with the Hebrew meaning of his last name (massa/burden) provoked this decades-long study—the result of which you hold in your hands. Mark passionately communicates how God's War Songs and War Dances against His enemies are available for our warfare. He wants you to learn how to use these divine WMD's from God's arsenal.

Married to his wife, Sharon, for over 35 years, together they have three sons: Mark-Aaron, Seth Josiah and Fredrick (Rick) James (married to Megan). They own a small ranch in Richardsville, KY, caring for four horses, three dogs and two cats.

Made in the USA
Middletown, DE
02 October 2021